SURVIVING HURRICANE MICHAEL

A Community's Story of Devastation, Survival and Hope during Recovery

by

Kay Keel Dennis

Surviving Hurricane Michael: A Community's Story of Devastation, Survival and Hope during Recovery

Copyright © 2019 by Kay Keel Dennis.

Front Cover Image by Scott Hagin..
Back Cover Image by Rhonda Dykes.

Printed in the United States of America

First Printing, December 2019

ISBN-9781670817778

Amazon Direct Publishing

For Ed.

This book is dedicated to the People in Marianna and surrounding area. All proceeds will be donated to the City of Marianna for recovery efforts.

A special thank you to all the first responders, churches and people in the community, who came together with hope and disregard for their own losses to help one another during the time of crisis and recovery.

Table of Contents

Introduction

Imagine living in a small town draped in natural beauty. A place where everywhere you go, you see someone you know, and they all feel like family. Visualize waking up to the sounds of birds chirping and going to bed listening to crickets. Envision spending weekends exploring caves and forests, and paddling and swimming in crystal clear springs. Imagine raising your children in a town where people look out for one another, and it's still fun to catch fireflies. Envision spending time with your children fishing on a beautiful river, whose sound and flow is mesmerizing. Visualize seeing your friends and family at church on Sunday mornings and at the ballpark on weeknights. Imagine driving down streets with canopy oaks dripping with Spanish moss with your windows down, so you can smell the magnolia blossoms. Envision lazily walking down the sidewalk decorated with shades of nature's green and being invited by a neighbor to enjoy a glass of sweet iced tea on their porch. Imagine being engulfed in history and a sense of place every time you leave your home. That's Marianna, a place I refer to as "heaven on earth".

Danny Pate teaching children how to fish at Hinson Conservation and Recreation Area. Photos provided by Kay Dennis.

Former Commissioner James Wise and Jackson Hospital staff celebrating Saint Patrick's Day Festivities. Photos provided by Kay Dennis.

Holiday window shopping and Christmas celebrations. Photos provided by
Kay Dennis

SURVIVING HURRICANE MICHAEL: A COMMUNITY'S STORY OF DEVASTATION, SURVIVAL AND HOPE DURING RECOVERY

Top: Dick Hinson and former City Commissioner Roger Clay. **Bottom**: Former City Commissioner Howard Milton signing a proclamation. Photos provided by Kay Dennis.

Photos provided by Kay Dennis.

SURVIVING HURRICANE MICHAEL: A COMMUNITY'S STORY OF DEVASTATION, SURVIVAL AND HOPE DURING RECOVERY

Top: Photo of Atamasco Lily taken at Hinson Conservation and Recreation Area. **Bottom**: Photo taken looking west from Yancey Bridge on Caverns Road in Marianna. Photos provided by Kay Dennis.

Top: Photo taken at Butler Recreation Area. **Bottom Left**: Photo taken at festival celebrating the trail openings at Hinson Conservation and Recreation Area. **Bottom Right**: Former Commissioner Paul Donofro, Jr. and Ann Hinson. Photos provided by Kay Dennis.

SURVIVING HURRICANE MICHAEL: A COMMUNITY'S STORY OF DEVASTATION, SURVIVAL AND HOPE DURING RECOVERY

Tim Gilley and Anna Dennis Gilley on their wedding day, May 11, 2013. Photos taken by Jerica Elizabeth Ward at Look and Tremble on the Chipola River. Photos provided by Kay Dennis.

Upper Left: Buffalo Soldier ceremony at Marry Marianna event in 2018. During the event, the citizens and other government agencies exchanged vows to work with one another and enjoyed wedding cake.

Middle Left: (left to right: Alan Ward, City Commissioner; Municipal Development Director Kay Dennis, AICP; Community Development Director, Wilanne Daniels; County Commissioner Eric Hill; City Manager Jim Dean; APA Program Manager Ryan Scherzinger, AICP; and APA volunteer Ellen Heath, FAICP.

Bottom Left: Stakeholder Meeting with APA Volunteers Tom Lavish; Peter Costa, AICP, PIP; and Mary Morton, AICP.

Photos provided by Kay Dennis.

SURVIVING HURRICANE MICHAEL: A COMMUNITY'S STORY OF DEVASTATION, SURVIVAL AND HOPE DURING RECOVERY

Historic Marianna. Photos provided by Kay Dennis.

Above: Retirement of Paul Donofro, Jr. after nearly three decades of service. From left to right: Commissioners Ephriam, Roberts, Donofro, Williams and Ward. **Below**: Ground breaking for Caledonia Street Parking Area. Below: Left to Right: Joseph Alday, Kay Dennis, Mary Gavin, Sam Everett, Richard Maychek, Commissioner Ephriam, Commissioner Hamilton, Charlotte Brunner, USDA RD Representative, and Chief Lovett. Photos provided by Jim Dean.

October 10th, 2018 at 2:00 pm the City of Marianna changed forever. Buildings standing firm and tall for centuries were suddenly empty doll-house structures. Monuments honoring military veterans and fallen war heroes were demolished in an instant. Every street in town and most homes were covered with huge trees. Communication stopped immediately. Citizens and visitors lost cellular and land-line phone, television and Internet connections, creating a feeling of isolation.

Being approximately seventy miles inland, most locals had lived through many hurricanes. The very worst storms remembered had some wind, random tornadoes and rain. Hurricane Michael would defy the odds, and make landfall so quickly that no one was prepared. Citizens cleaned off the shelves of the local stores the night before the storm, but most only had enough supplies to last a couple of days. That was more than was usually required. The four to six hour period the eye wall passed over Marianna looked like a blizzard. Seeing past the end of one's arm was nearly impossible, due to the whiteout conditions. Many ventured out during the middle of the eye, only to find the worst of the storm was yet to come. Others never saw the eye, and endured the solid eye-wall. Assistance would only be available after streets were cleared. Two days following the storm, purchasing fuel for a generator meant paying cash and traveling 60 miles or more through dangerous paths of fallen power poles and trees.

How could a small rural town possibly recover from the physical and emotional effects of Hurricane Michael? Almost immediately fire and police officers from around the country arrived to assist locals and keep citizens safe. Utility and road crews from everywhere imaginable began helping to clean-up and restore electrical services nonstop around the clock. Neighbors helped neighbors recover family and friends trapped within their homes. First responders were sent out as areas became clear. People from all types of relief organizations brought food, clothing, and other supplies to the needy. The community rallied and continue to rally together to help one another, all thankful to have survived Hurricane Michael.

Living seventy miles inland from the coast usually provides safety from hurricanes. Yet, there are times when the unexpected occurs. As a certified urban planner with more than twenty-two years of experience in planning, greenway management, code enforcement, grant writing and management, I was caught off guard by Hurricane Michael. How does an economically depressed area with a housing shortage recover? This book will provide guidance for people who may encounter similar unexpected disasters, while documenting history as recorded through heart-felt stories of survivors. While the shared stories denote bravery at the highest level, I felt and saw the pain of each person I interviewed. I also have a story, and have been involved in recovery. I found similarities and differences with mine in each. Keep in mind, these are just a few of the stories provided by area residents. Everyone in the community endured Hurricane Michael in one way or another, but each story reveals new depths of understanding.

Recovery takes time, money, people and action. While there is no way to prevent a hurricane from impacting your life, you can be prepared. Do not wait until you are in the middle of a disaster to come up with a plan.

Photo provided by Rhonda Dykes.

PART I

The Storm Is Coming

Photo provided by Terry Cole at WMBB.

O n the first day of October in 2018 area residents learned of a low-pressure area forming in the southwestern Caribbean Sea. People living in Florida are always aware of tropical storm activity and hurricanes, but do not typically overreact when they first hear about storms forming. These types of storms are unpredictable and tend to vary in intensity. In Marianna, residents usually have some hurricane supplies on hand and are aware when it is hurricane season. However, history shows damage associated with hurricanes or tropical storms in Marianna and Jackson County has been limited to flooding and random tornadic activity. Historic hurricane activity in the area was for the storm to weaken as it approached landfall.

Within seven days Hurricane Michael was near Cuba and moving northward. That's when developments began to take place more quickly with the hurricane strengthening in the Gulf of Mexico. On October 9th Hurricane Michael was predicted to make landfall about 60 miles south of Marianna as a major hurricane. The attention of locals was raised, but most knew of the Sand Hill bluffs south of town that were believed to divert storm damage from the area.

Chief Meteorologist Ross Whitley sharing what the radar looked like on the morning of Monday, October 8, 2018 at 4:09 a.m. Photos provided by Terry Cole at WMBB.

Chief Meteorologist Ross Whitley explaining conditions on the morning of Tuesday, October 9, 2018 at 4:00 a.m. Photos provided by Terry Cole at WMBB.

Some say complacency may have settled on the historic town known for antebellum homes and its pristine natural environment. However, local businesses and government officials began to ensure families were allowed to go home and make preparations just in case there was more.

Chief Meteorologist Ross Whitley updating viewers on conditions Tuesday evening October 9, 2018 at 7:00 p.m. – the night before Hurricane Michael made landfall. Photo provided by Terry Cole at WMBB.

SURVIVING HURRICANE MICHAEL: A COMMUNITY'S STORY OF DEVASTATION, SURVIVAL AND HOPE DURING RECOVERY

On Tuesday evening the weather situation was starting to look serious. Yet, it was late in the game to evacuate. While the storm had most people's attention, being trapped on the road was dangerous. For many there was that little voice saying "the storm will lose intensity and turn when it starts touching land".

Wednesday, October 10, 2018 at 5:00 a.m. – the day Hurricane Michael made landfall Ross Whitley updating viewers. Photo provided by Terry Cole at WMBB.

Wednesday, October 10, 2018 at 9:00 a.m. – the day Hurricane Michael made landfall Ross Whitley provided updates. Photo provided by Terry Cole at WMBB.

Mid-morning on Wednesday, October 10, 2018 Ross Whitley pointing out details about Hurricane Michael. Photos provided by Terry Cole at WMBB

When Wednesday morning arrived, seriousness set it. It was too late to leave town. The one shelter open to the general public was filling up. At this point it was a waiting game. Most would sit in front of their television sets anticipating weather updates, which were constant by this time. Many would watch until the local stations were no longer available and the power was out. Updates would become harder to find with cellular signal losses, land-lines down and lack of Internet service. It was a waiting game that would be disaster for many.

Photo provided by Terry Cole at WMBB.

Chapter One
Is It Serious?

Seriousness varies from person to person based on experience and longevity in the area. Some people changed their opinion on the seriousness of the storm as it rapidly approached. Others remained skeptical. Regardless, each person would soon learn just how serious a category five hurricane could be.

Photos taken during Hurricane Michael and provided by Douglas Rorex.

Father David Green

Father David Green, Reverend of Saint Luke's Episcopal Church in Marianna, grew up in Mobile, Alabama and lived in Gulf Shores, Alabama for 28 years. "I'd been around hurricanes all my life and ridden out some really bad ones," he shared. In fact, he recalled in some cases evacuating. One of the worst storms Father David remembered occurred when he lived in Mobile, and Hurricane Frederic came up Mobile Bay. At that time he and his wife Charlotte were newlyweds, and were without electrical power for 19 days. Father David shared how Hurricane Frederic blew away the town of Gulf Shores, which he would later call home.

In 2004 Father David survived Hurricane Ivan, which created mass destruction in Gulf Shores, including his furniture store building. "Then, the following year Katrina came, and I had two daughters living in New Orleans" he shared. "In all my years, I never, never expected for a hurricane to be that strong so far inland."

Historic Saint Luke's Episcopal Church before Hurricane Michael.
Photo provided by Kay Dennis.

Father David admittedly didn't take the storm that seriously. "I was thinking we were so far away from the water that it would weaken by the time it got here." He recalled watching the news the morning Hurricane Michael was to make landfall and still thinking it wouldn't be that bad.

Before the power went out, Father David and Charlotte took food out of the freezer and put it on ice, and filled up the bathtubs with water. He explained that they had supplies that would last a while. Father David, Charlotte and their dog prepared to ride out the storm. "I didn't have any idea that the eye of the storm was going to go right over our house!"

Reverend Ronald Mizer

Father David was not alone. Many other people felt the same way. Reverend Ronald Mizer, Pastor at Saint James AME Church, shared, "people weren't as intimidated with the concept of a storm of that nature coming through Jackson County until the day before, when it was reported Marianna would take a direct hit." Reverend Mizer elaborated, "as a community of faith we tried to make sure people knew what was going to transpire and were prepared." "Many were unaware that it would actually be like this," Reverend Mizer added. He explained how he lost power at about 12:30 p.m., and the radio didn't pick up well after that.

Pastor Kevin Yoder

Kevin Yoder, Pastor of Adult Ministries at Rivertown Community Church, also decided to stay home. Kevin decided to make preparations to ride out the storm. His wife's family was traveling in for a visit from Pennsylvania the same week. Despite Kevin and Lisa's attempts to convince them to postpone their trip, they came in early. "Wednesday morning we heard the storm was predicted to be a category four, so we hunkered down in our brick home," Kevin explained.

Ann Jones

Business owners may have been skeptical, but seemed to prepare cautiously. Local realtor Ann Jones shared that she didn't worry until the day before the storm when Verizon's corporate office called her seeking staging areas for temporary cellular towers. "Then another guy wanted to bring about fifteen big trucks and I found him a place to park them," she continued. She secured listed real estate properties and pulled up realtor signs in preparation. "When I arrived home my grandson helped me secure our house," she added, "by roping the garbage can around a tree, storing the kayak in the shed, and moving vehicles to my office, and under the power-lines away from trees."

Georgeann Adkison

Similarly, Georgeann Adkison, Financial Center Manager, AVP with Hancock Whitney Bank, explained how her company has procedures and teams set up in Texas, Louisiana, Florida, Alabama, Mississippi and throughout the footprint of the organization. The Headquarters for Hancock Whitney is Gulfport, Mississippi. "They learned from Hurricane Katrina," Georgeann explained. "We stayed open until the end of the day before the storm, and then went into standby," she continued. "We have a communication mechanism with the bank." "The night before I went home," Georgeann shared, "I wasn't expecting anything that bad." "In fact, I had been talking to friends and family about enjoying a day off together," she explained. "That night several families went to a mutual friend's farm with our children, because we just weren't expecting anything serious."

Elizabeth Simpson

Local Attorney Elizabeth Milton Simpson's office is located immediately north of the Jackson County Court House in downtown Marianna. Elizabeth is the Assistant Public Defender, where she works felony cases and cases for Sunland Training Center, especially when the clients need medical procedures and

8

medications. She has been a lawyer for many years working in the Public Defender's Office, with juveniles and a general law practice where she has done a little of everything such as divorces, paternity, adoptions, and similar legal matters. "I wanted to be an attorney, so I could help people," she explained. Not only is Elizabeth an attorney, but she married an attorney, and together they have two beautiful and intelligent daughters. Elizabeth shared how the day before Hurricane Michael hit that she had learned her husband, John had cancer again. This was eight days before the couples thirty-third anniversary. The couple decided to ride out the storm at their home.

Jay James

Jay James, hometown girl and business owner, described how she was swimming in her aunt's pool the Saturday before the storm arrived. "On Sunday I began listening and by Monday, I started paying attention and preparing," she explained. On Tuesday Jay and her daughter evacuated to stay with family on the north side of town. Her husband, mother-in-law, dog and pig stayed at their home to weather the storm.

Joan Schairer

On Tuesday night before the storm Joan Schairer shared that she watched the Weather Channel and listened to a discussion about a category two hurricane in the Gulf of Mexico. While she understood there would be bad weather, she decided to hunker down within her home on top of a hill just south of the City limits of Marianna. Wednesday morning Joan went about her normal routine and sat down with her coffee to see Jim Cantore standing on the beach in Mexico Beach, which is about 70 miles south of Marianna. "I had two words, 'Oh Shit!'" Joan shared. At that time the discussion on television was Hurricane Michael was a category three and possibly a four at landfall. "It looked like Mexico Beach was either going to be in the eye or very near it," she described. Joan secured the outside of her home, placing anything that might fly away in the garage with her truck. Joan had supplies and water. There were no trees in Joan's yard. However, there were too many trees to count on the parcel immediately to her west and north.

Joan Schairer's home before Hurricane Michael. Photo provided by Joan Schairer

Joan's mother, Lois, was at Marianna Health and Rehab learning to walk again after recent health issues. So, she also secured her mother's home on the east side of town, and parked her mother's vehicle in the garage the day before.

Melissa Krebeck

Other people in the community had mixed reactions, as well. Resident and single mother of two, Melissa Krebeck, took the storm seriously. Melissa, a "Boy Scout Mom", is someone who enjoys and frequently camps. So, she had can goods and nonperishables already on hand. However, she filled a 50 gallon barrel that she had outside with water just in case. "Monday night I realized the storm was a big deal, but I didn't want to worry the kids," She shared. Tuesday, Melissa went about her normal routine of working the food pantry at a local church before she was given the remainder of the day off to make last minute preparations.

Royce Reagan

Royce Reagan thought the storm would be bad, "but we decided to stay and wing it," he shared optimistically. Royce's wooden house was constructed with 12 inch wide Board and Batten. "It was half old house and half new house," he clarified to explain that the house had a newer addition. His home was beautifully placed near the Chipola River and surrounded by a tree buffer that provided complete privacy.

Royce and Jackie Reagan's home before Hurricane Michael. Photo provided by Royce Reagan.

Michelle Borden

Michelle Borden grew up in Fort Lauderdale and was no stranger to hurricanes. "This is not my first hurricane and I joke that it probably won't be my last," Michelle shared. Yet, Michelle described Hurricane Michael as the worst Hurricane she had survived. As a young teen Michelle lived in south Florida when Hurricane Andrew hit, but she was on a cruise the day Andrew made landfall. She had seen many hurricanes. "I went to school in south Florida, when Wilma and Katrina went back and forth

11

over a ten day period, which were category three hurricanes when they hit us," she continued.

Although Michelle moved to Marianna in 2015, she had purchased a home on West Manor Street only three months prior to the storm. When preparing for Hurricane Michael, Michelle explained, "I thought it was going to be a category three." Her previous experience with category three hurricanes was she needed to get some water and prepare for loss of electricity. While her children were with their father the night before, Michelle and her boyfriend went out to dinner to celebrate her 40th birthday, which was October 10th. "That's when we heard that it might be a four," she shared.

Michelle recalled how she woke up on her birthday with multiple messages and calls on her cell phone. "I was thinking what the heck is going on, and it must be birthday texts," she continued. Someone told her to call her mom, who lived in Fort Meyers Beach, to let her mom know what was going on. Michelle's mother cried and tried to convince her to evacuate, but Michelle simply explained to her mother that the storm was a category three and would die down once it hit land. After all, this is what usually took place. Michelle's mother had evacuated to Marianna when Hurricane Irma came through where she lived. Still having hurricane related anxiety, Michelle's mother pleaded with her to leave, especially since her children were too young to be exposed to this type of disaster. However, Michelle continued to explain, "Mom, it's just a category three and it will probably die down by the time it gets to us." Michelle was not alone thinking that there would be wind, rain, a few fallen trees and power outages. "I had three dead trees in my yard and I was thinking, they will go down and I won't have to pay to get them removed anymore," she jokingly shared.

Michelle and her boyfriend downloaded movies on the tablets of her four year old son and seven year old daughter. Then, she gathered up games and puzzles, knowing they had non-perishable food and drinking water on hand. "My kids love the frozen peanut butter and jelly sandwiches, and I thought if they defrost, so what." She explained to her children that they probably wouldn't have Internet, but they had games and puzzles for fun during that time. "In my head I thought we'd probably be out of power for 48 hours, and that's all I planned for," she recalled. They decided to ride out the storm in her new home.

It has always been common for locals to pay attention to the weather during hurricane season and make preparations as needed. This storm was different from anything seen by those living in Marianna. Some were afraid and scampering around. Others did not take it serious enough. While meteorologists have more scientific knowledge and technology to let citizens know strength and landfall of storms, there is no way for locals to predict the outcome.

Paula Livergood

Prior to the storm Paula and her family had some supplies on hand. "I thought maybe a few days to a week is all we needed" Paula shared. Paula starting feeling some fear the day before the storm thinking it could get bad. As she watched weather reports, Paula came across an app for her cell phone that allowed the user to input their address. "That's when I realized the storm would go directly over my house," Paula explained. Paula shared how when Hurricane Noah was headed toward Marianna, she had picked up and secured everything in the yard only to find out it wasn't necessary. So, this time she wasn't quite as thorough. Paula went to the store to purchase a generator and a couple of containers of gas. "Still, I wasn't fully prepared for how big an impact the storm would make on my life," she shared. Not knowing how much to prepare for in terms of supplies was a common problem. When asked if she had ever been through a storm like this before, Paula responded "no, this was my first rodeo."

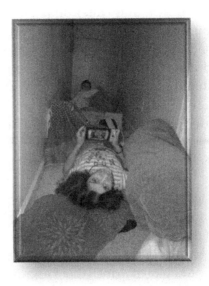

Carlton and Danielle Livergood prepared to ride out Hurricane Michael in the hall of their home. Photo provided by Paula Livergood.

Since every single room in Paula's house has windows, the day of the storm Paula began taking cushions off the furniture and moving them to the hallway upstairs, where she could shut off other rooms to the house. Paula's teens Danielle and Carlton went with her to the hallway and brought with them games to occupy their time. Paula's mom, Julia Hodges, stayed alone in the basement below with a couple of their dogs.

Shelby Durham

Shelby and her husband Matthew moved to Jackson County in 2007, before relocating to the Deer Point Lake area in 2016, where they could work in Panama City. The weekend before Hurricane Michael made landfall, Shelby and Matthew came through Marianna on their way to a rodeo in Bonifay. "I remember sitting at the rodeo and Matthew saying 'oh we're going to have a tropical storm this weekend,'" she recalled thinking that they would have some rain.

The couple returned to work as usual in Panama City on Monday. Then, Matthew made the decision to board up the house and secure things. When he asked Shelby about packing to leave for his parent's home in Marianna, she was caught off guard. "I said 'Matthew I just feel like it's not going to do anything,'" she shared. Despite not feeling the necessity to leave town, she packed Monday night. After working half a day on Tuesday, the couple left town to stay at his parent's home in Marianna on Tuesday night. The next morning Matthew heard a news report indicating that Hurricane Michael would hit Marianna as a category four storm. So, the family loaded up their belongings and left town. They evacuated with their dogs to Tuscaloosa, Alabama.

Ronnie Keel

Ronnie Keel was certainly no different from others in Marianna. "The weather reports are grossly exaggerated, so I wasn't expecting it to be near as bad as it was," explained Ronnie Keel, a life-long resident of Jackson County who has lived in Marianna the majority of his life. "I would have stayed if I had known it was going to be that bad, because it didn't make any difference," he continued. Ronnie explained that his wife, youngest daughter and her children had left for Tennessee on Wednesday morning. His son and daughter-in-law were in Panama City riding out the storm, and his oldest daughter and her family were across town. Ronnie would ride out the storm alone. He didn't even prepare with supplies. "I just opened the door, so I could see what was going on, and that was about the size of it," Ronnie shared.

James Lash

The home of James and Catherine Lash before Hurricane Michael. Photo provided by their daughter, Debbie Lash Lollie.

Ronnie Keel's next door neighbors are James and Catherine Lash. If you ever meet James Lash, don't let his energy fool you. This ninety year old man and his 87 year old wife of 71 years, decided to ride out a category five hurricane together. He shared how he didn't think the weather was going to be that bad. Having been through so many storms, and knowing the difficulties of moving his bedridden wife, James decided to stay home. One of the issues with transporting Catherine was she would have to go from a wheelchair to a van. So, James set up his 5000 watt generator, and then purchased a gas cooker and fuel for it. He gathered up lanterns, candles and flashlights, and had them available for use. Then, his son-in-law, Ronnie Lollie, came over and stayed with him. "If he hadn't been there, I wouldn't have stood a prayer," James shared. He didn't purchase any food, because he had plenty of canned goods and food in his freezer.

Ronstance Pittman

Ronstance, a fitness trainer at Chipola Fitness and president of the local NAACP chapter, recalls a couple of days before Hurricane Michael made landfall realizing the seriousness of the storm after Jackson County Emergency Management Director, Rodney Andreasen addressed the community. She immediately picked up batteries, water, food and other supplies. However, she recalled the one item they didn't have was a generator.

In fact, she remembers her new husband of only a couple of months, Roger, and daughter, Shaleigh, were laughing at her. Ronstance's mother came to stay with them the night before the storm bringing salmon salad. Ronstance secured everything outside her home and then, made sure her dog, Coco had food and water. She had her daughter fill up her bathtub with water, meanwhile they continued laughing at her.

Shaleigh, recalled a slightly different story at a Tropicana Speech Contest where she won second place. Shaleigh shared that her mother was unplugging the electronics, while she was filling the bathtub with water. Shaleigh continued, "my grandmother was telling my mom to calm down, even though she was the one sitting in the bathroom praying." Ronstance and her family decided against evacuation.

Carmen Smith

Carmen Smith, Executive Director of Habitat for Humanity in Jackson and Washington Counties, is a highly intellectual young woman. However, she was caught off guard by what was to occur. Carmen's maternal aunt had passed away only eight days before Hurricane Michael made landfall. Carmen was in Saint Petersburg, Florida on Sunday when she saw the news. Carmen had originally planned to leave on Monday, but decided to return home. "Still I didn't think what was to transpire was going to happen," she shared. Carmen explained how she knew to prepare, but did not know to what extent. Carmen picked up her grandmother to take her along with her, her fiancé and two dogs to Tallahassee to her parent's home on Tuesday. While she was uncertain at the time, it turned out to be a wise decision for Carmen and her family.

As the time of landfall approached television radar images displayed a perfect and beautiful storm. It suddenly appeared that this storm was different from all others. The intensity was strengthening and the pressure continued to drop. There comes a point in time with hurricane evacuation, when it is too dangerous to be out on the road. Often traffic is moving slowly, if at all. Television personalities began instructing their audiences to "hunker down," if they had not already left the area. Residents in mobile homes and low lying areas were told to seek shelter. Rules regarding pets, medications and special needs were being repeated strongly. Some residents and visitors left. Others decided to stay and ride out the storm. That is when the waiting game began. Hurricane Michael would exceed all expectations.

Richard Williams

Richard Williams, Executive Director of CareerSource Chipola and Executive Director of Opportunity Florida, shared that he was tracking the storm in advance. Richard was away from the office at meetings in Blountstown and Chipley prior to the storm. However, he thought that they would be able to return to work on Friday.

Kenny Griffin

Kenny Griffin, Director of Business Services at CareerSource Chipola, explained that he really didn't think the weather would be that bad. "In fact, when we let the employees leave on Tuesday, I said 'see you Thursday,'" Kenny added. His thoughts were possibly power outages for a couple of days and a few limbs down. "I still thought up to the last, that maybe 100 mile per hour winds," he continued. Kenny admitted that he never considered he would see in his lifetime what actually happened.

Betty Demmon

Betty Demmon explained how the day before the storm made landfall, the WJAQ FM station was on the air via satellite. Once the office was secure, the employees were allowed to go home to prepare for the unknown. She had no idea what was to follow or what an important role she would have during the aftermath of Hurricane Michael.

While there were varying opinions in Marianna on what to expect, no one ever really knows what type of weather a hurricane will bring. Some seem severe, but bring only rain. Others seem less severe, and dangerous tornadoes spin off the storm. The lack of knowledge and unpredictability lead to complacency among Floridians. Despite local opinions, City and County officials knew they needed to be ready for whatever was to come, even if it was a false alarm. Public safety and welfare became a priority as time progressed.

Chapter Two
Preparing for the Unknown

Rumblings of preparations began to fill City Hall, especially by people new to the area or from out-of-town. The old-timers and natives to Marianna chuckled to themselves about the conversations taking place, while preparing for what they thought would be rain, wind and at the very worst, a small tornado. While they knew this was serious, they had no way of knowing what was ahead of them.

John Roberts, Mayor/City Commissioner

John Roberts was the Mayor of the City of Marianna, when Hurricane Michael came through town. On Saturday, four days before the storm, Mayor Roberts was with his family at Panama City Beach. He even shared that his wife, Kathryn went swimming in the Gulf. The weather was nice on Saturday, which gives an indication of the amount of time locals had to prepare before landfall. At first, the Mayor admittedly thought it was just going to be another tropical storm. However, as they watched the news, the storm continued to grow. "I never dreamed that it would be strong enough to do the damage that it did inland" he shared. "My father always told me that we didn't have a lot to worry about, because we were 70 miles inland," he continued. "He said 'after it hit the coast it would be slowed down by the time it got to Marianna,' but he never dreamed it would hit the coast going 160 miles per hour." Hurricane Michael would have 160 miles per hour sustained winds with wind gusts exceeding that amount.

Rico Williams, City Commissioner

Although Commissioner Williams was not Mayor when Hurricane Michael came through Marianna, he was a City Commissioner and would be Mayor eight months into the recovery. Commissioner Williams remembered anticipating a bad storm was coming. "I talked to my son saying 'look around you,'" he continued, "'you'll never see Marianna like this again.'" Commissioner Williams took his family to stay with his parents, because he needed the peace of mind knowing that they were okay. Commissioner Williams foresaw the difficulties there would be in him trying to go across town to check on his parents after the storm.

Jim Dean, City Manager

"I made some minor preparations at home, and around noon on October 9th, I sent employees home out of precaution" City Manager, Jim Dean explained. This turned out to be a wise idea, because the stores were out of many needed supplies. Lines were long in stores and at gas stations. Jim continued working.

Public Works

Similarly, Joe Richey, Public Works Director for the City of Marianna, anticipated a catastrophic storm. Under Joe's direction, Rick Harrell, City of Marianna Water and Waste Water Supervisor, explained how he immediately registered with

FlaWARN, which is sponsored by the Florida Department of Environmental Protection. Rick clarified "FlaWARN is an organization, where cities through water and wastewater supervisors can respond to disasters." Also under the direction of Joe, Douglas Glass, Natural Gas Supervisor registered with the Florida Natural Gas Association for a similar type of assistance. "The day of the storm, I put all the City of Marianna wells on generators," Rick continued. Meanwhile, Doug checked all the generators and went through natural disaster procedures on Wednesday. Joe ensured the loader, a piece of heavy equipment, was parked on a vacant lot at City Hall and vehicles were fueled.

Sam Everett, Supervisor of Streets, Facilities and Fleet Maintenance, viewed Hurricane Michael as a serious threat to the community. He was in Miami, when Hurricane Andrew made landfall in 1992, and explained "I understand the gravity of a cat four or category five storm". He took down all the trees in his yard long before the storm arrived, because he knew Marianna was a "Tree City," with trees decorating every street in town. Sam went beyond removing his own trees to warning others in the City that if a large storm came through, the potential number of trees to fall would make the storm catastrophic for the community. Sam believed Marianna had an excessive amount of trees. "Even with a small storm, there would be six to eight trees down, limbs would fall off and break," he continued. "This would wreak havoc on people having electricity and fallen limbs causing wrecks" he continued. "Working in the field allows you to see things from a different perspective," Sam explained. However, the locals did not heed his warnings, because they loved the beautiful trees.

Sam originally thought his family could ride out the storm at home, but he prepared by loading his truck with storm lights, a chainsaw, oil, chains and other supplies. His preparations were made to ensure he could return to help the citizens of Marianna. When Sam arose on Wednesday, October 10, 2018, he turned on his television to learn that Hurricane Michael was a category four and expected to be a category five. He quickly woke up everyone in his house. When his family fussed about leaving, he told them "quick, get up because hell is on the way and we gotta get out of here!" Sam took his family to Marianna High School, which had been designated at storm shelter.

Charlie Curry, who works under Sam's supervision operating the City's clam truck, called Sam. Sam shared that when he told Charlie that he was going to the storm shelter, "Charlie said 'boss if you are going to the storm shelter, I'm taking my family and going too.'" "My first priority was to get my family to a safe location, because I knew that with my job, whatever happened, I was going to be out on the streets." Sam's family took their dog, Semi (short for Seminole), with them.

Sam, also a minister, had much on his mind that day: the needs of his family, his congregation, his own needs and his City's needs. "All of these things were developing in my mind and I was balancing it with the grace of God," he shared. Sam had instructed his congregation on the previous Sunday to be prepared with supplies and seek shelter if necessary, especially if residing in a mobile home. "The biggest sentiment at that time with Marianna skirting storms so many times was 'well, you know pastor we've had this before and it always turned away before it got to us,'" he shared.

Since the shelter did not have any televisions, people staying were informed with radios. "There is always a calm before the storm," Sam explained. He remembered looking at the television at home knowing Hurricane Michael would be a monster that would not turn away from Marianna.

Hayes Baggett, Chief of Police

Meanwhile on Sunday morning, Hayes Baggett, City of Marianna Chief of Police, noticed there was a tropical depression and he had only two days to prepare. On Monday, Chief Baggett requested the City's Network Administrator, Ron Swift, check the generators for City Hall and the Police Station. That's when they discovered there was a problem with one of the generators working. Though the repair was made, on Tuesday, Ron was called back again, because the generator for the Police Station was still not working properly. Finally, it cranked and would continue to run for three weeks. "We didn't turn it off," Chief Baggett explained. "It was divine intervention that no one had to repair it." Meanwhile, Nick Stroud, Investigative Lieutenant for the Marianna Police Department, ensured there were plenty of plugs for tires available. This turned out to be more help than they could anticipate.

Captain Clint Watson, Fire Marshall, and Captain Brice Phillips - Marianna Fire Department

Captain Clint Watson, City of Marianna Fire Marshall, has lived in Marianna all his life. Knowing Marianna doesn't usually take a direct hit, he initially didn't get too concerned. Then, he noticed the storm was developing quickly. "We had limited time and a job to do," he explained. Evacuating was not an option in his position at the City of Mariana Fire Department.

Brice Phillips also with the Marianna Fire Department shared how he went to bed thinking Hurricane Michael was going to be a category two hurricane. At the station they discussed the situation and initially thought everything would be okay. "The day of the storm you wake up and you have nowhere to go," Brice added. The opportunity to evacuate has come and gone.

Melinda Gay, Marianna Health and Rehab Administrator

Marianna Health and Rehabilitation Administrator, Melinda Gay explained how she took the storm seriously. "I ordered extra supplies, filled the storage tank and topped off the generator, before I began preparing staff to shelter in place." Melinda's advance preparations would prove beneficial for residents, staff and their families for days ahead.

Kim Johnson Applewhite, City Clerk/Finance Director

Kim Applewhite, City of Marianna Clerk and Finance Director for the City of Marianna, and Grand Ridge City Council Member, lives in Grand Ridge, which is only about ten or fifteen minutes away from Marianna. She shared that her daughter had evacuated with her grandson, but she, not thinking it would be as bad as it was, decided to stay at her mother's home with her husband, mother and son because there weren't many trees around. "I'm glad she left with the baby because a tree went through her house," Kim shared. "We wouldn't never do that again," she added.

Clay Wells, Parks and Recreation Director

Clay Wells, City of Marianna Parks and Recreation Director, grew up just across the state line in Georgia, but always attended school in Florida. Clay and his wife, Crystle, moved to Chattahoochee in 2001. The storm came up quickly and the couple thought they'd get some rough winds, and it would be like all the other storms that had previously come through the area. "I figured a power outage for seven or eight hours, a few trees and stuff like that," Clay shared. While he didn't take the storm too seriously, Clay did purchase a few supplies. The couple decided to stay at their home in Chattahoochee, because of Crystle's supervisory position over purchasing for the warehouse at Florida State Hospital.

Jimmy Grant, Building Official

"I thought it wouldn't be bad, because this had never happened before," explained Building Official Jimmy Grant. "We didn't spend a lot of time preparing," Jimmy continued. "We were acting like our heads were in the sand!" Jimmy explained how the storm came up quickly, and he had worked hard the day before. "I thought about going fishing," he admitted. This sentiment has been reiterated repeatedly.

Wilanne Daniels, Jackson County Administrator

Interim County Administrator, Wilanne Daniels had a six-week old baby and was on maternity leave, but working from home, when she received a call that there was going to be a "little storm". On Monday, October 8th a Board of County Commissioners' Meeting was called to declare a State of Emergency. This was also Wilanne's first day back after maternity leave. Immediately following the meeting, she met with the Emergency Management Director and decided to close the County offices at noon the following day to provide employees a little extra time to prepare for the storm. Wilanne stayed at the Emergency Operations Center (EOC) until early evening with her six week old baby to keep an eye on events as they unfolded.

Wilanne, her husband, Ryan and three small children lodged with family in Marianna, so they would be close to the Emergency Operations Center. She returned to the Emergency Operations Center on Wednesday until it was time to go home and prepare for the storm. "The expectation was it would be like anything else we have experienced in my lifetime," Wilanne recalled. "To be honest, even as it continued to grow in strength and to grow stronger, I had no point of reference to what kind of destruction and how bad this hurricane could be," she continued. "I had never been to an area following a storm like that, and I had no understanding of how severe it could be."

Sergeant Martin Basford, Jackson County Sheriff's Department

Martin Basford, Sergeant and Supervisor of Jackson County Courthouse Security, had never been alarmed by the weather. "I just didn't think much of it," he shared. Martin's son helped him to secure their Grand Ridge home and he took his three sons and wife to stay with his father, who lived near Chipola College in Marianna. When Martin went to work on hurricane shift at 5 a.m. October 10th, he began to realize the severity of what was to come as he listened to reports on the radio. "I picked up my family and took them to the Chipola College Public Service Building," he recalled. The Public Service Building had been established as a shelter for first responders and their families. Martin loaded up his chainsaw and some other equipment in his County vehicle just in case it was needed.

Corporal Michael Mears, Jackson County Sheriff's Department

Michel Mears, a supervisor at the Jackson County Sheriff's Department, thought it would be a rough storm, but not as bad as it turned out. "Watching the weather reports, they said it could be a category three storm, but as it got into the Gulf it kept building, building and building," he explained. Mike shared that at work, everyone was preparing for the unknown. "The morning of the storm it was real eerie feeling, almost like a calm," he shared.

Mason Brock, Florida Public Utilities

Mason Brock, Energy Conservation Specialist and Sales Representative with Florida Public Utilities, admitted that at first he thought Hurricane Michael probably wasn't a big deal. He went to work, attended Emergency Operation Center meetings and began making preparations. At midnight on the day of the storm, Mason watched the news from the Emergency Operations Center. Two hours later he called his family and friends and told them to evacuate. "I sent my family to the first responder's shelter at Chipola College, where the Florida Highway Patrol were stationed," he explained.

Kevin Daniel, Jackson Hospital

Everyone wasn't in town when they heard about Hurricane Michael. Kevin Daniel, Engineering Director for Jackson Hospital, explained how he was at a conference in Orlando. "People were getting called back, so I returned the night before and went to work the morning of October 10th." Kevin continued, "we moved fast to prepare and essential personnel stayed at the hospital."

Tiffany Garling, Executive Director, Jackson County Chamber of Commerce

As the storm was headed toward the Florida Panhandle, there were other events taking place. Tiffany Garling, Executive Director of the Jackson County Chamber of Commerce, shared how she and a colleague had been preparing for the annual Chamber Golf Tournament. "We finished up mid-day Friday and went to the Emergency Operations Center, where we remained most of the day to provide information and hurricane supplies to local business owners." When she woke up Sunday morning, Tiffany noticed the progression of the storm. "I texted the Jackson County Emergency Management Director, to find out about the conference call at the Emergency Operations Center," Tiffany recalled. "After I listened to the State conference call, I knew the seriousness facing Jackson County." Tiffany remembered that although she took the storm seriously, because of what she knew about Hurricane Irma, she had no idea what they were facing. Tuesday night Tiffany's family evacuated. Her fiancé remained, because of his responsibilities with a local business. The following morning the couple went to the Emergency Operations Center together.

As the time moved forward Hurricane Michael quickly gained intensity. Those who may have evacuated found it was too late. Riding out a hurricane at home is dangerous. In the event that there is a need for emergency help, residents hunkering down at home may find that assistance is unavailable due to the inability of first responders to respond.

PART II

The Storm Is Here

No matter how much you prepare, the inevitable always happens. Sometimes the wait is worse than what is anticipated. However, Hurricane Michael would prove itself more intense than anyone's wait time. The storm would take over the area for what seemed like four to six hours. Most locals lost track of time, or at least the memory of how long the storm lasted. Time would stand still in the minds of the people in Marianna and Jackson County. During this period of intense shock, the town was devastated.

Many of those who experienced the eye of the storm thought the storm was over. Others realized there was more to come. Still others never saw the eye, because they were experiencing the intensity of the eye wall for hours.

Once the worst of the storm had passed through the area, there was an intense need to see what had taken place. Yet, many would find themselves trapped and unable to leave their homes for days. Cabin Fever is real and isolation plays tricks with one's mind.

Regardless to individual situations, most were in a state of shock that would last not only days, but months to come

Chapter Three
Landfall

October 10, 2018 is a date that is etched in the memory of the residents of Marianna. Hurricane Michael made landfall near Mexico Beach as a category five hurricane with sustained winds of at least 160 miles per hour and gusts that were higher. Not only would Hurricane Michael be the strongest hurricane of the 2018 season, but it was third-most intense Atlantic hurricane to strike the United States in terms of pressure, the first category five hurricane to hit the Florida panhandle and the fourth-strongest land falling hurricane in the United States in terms of winds. [12]

Around 2 p.m. Hurricane Michael struck Marianna, which can be seen on the town clock that stopped with the storm's

---

[1] From "Hurricane Michael," by Wikipedia contributors, 2019, *Wikipedia, The Free Encyclopedia*.

[2] From "Hurricane Michael Makes Landfall in Florida Panhandle," by J. Masters, J., 2018.

arrival. Residents watched whiteout conditions and debris flying through the air. Unlike other hurricanes that lost intensity when making landfall, Michael plowed through Marianna severely damaging commercial buildings, homes, and churches. Every road in Jackson County was covered with trees making mobilization and rescue impossible. During the storm eye people looked around thinking the worse had already occurred. However, for most the back side of the storm offered even greater destruction than the front.

Father David Green

According to Father David, the wind blew out of the east and he believed a house closely located on the east side provided his home some protection. "It blew like all get out for two hours and then it got calmer," he shared. "I thought 'okay, it has passed and it's over.'" He and Charlotte stepped outside to assess the damage, and they noticed other neighbors doing the same. "Then, I realized the wind was shifting and it was starting to come out of the west," he continued. "I said 'oh my gosh! I'm in the eye of the storm.'" "I'd never been in the eye of a hurricane before," he added. Father David recalled seeing trees down all over the neighborhood. "We went back inside and had another two hours of hellacious wind," he added. Then, they begin to notice the window panes in their house vibrating and shaking. The couple made their way to the kitchen in the middle of the house. "We held up in there and did some praying," Father David continued. "It was bad," he firmly stated and paused. "It was bad," Father David repeated. After the storm calmed down, the couple went outside again. "The house two doors down had huge pine trees in it that had crushed the roof," he shared. "Other houses only about 100 yards down the street had multiple trees in them,"

Father David continued. "You couldn't have driven out for the trees blocking the road."

David and Charlotte Green's home after Hurricane Michael. Photo provided by Father David Green

Reverend Ronald Mizer

Reverend Mizer recalled how when the eye came through it was quiet, providing him an opportunity to survey the damage. "It was unbelievable," he shared, "like a war scene." Reverend Mizer noted damaged trees, blocked roads, and loss of electricity. Then, he started trying to come up with a new plan on how to survive and recover.

Pastor Kevin Yoder

While Kevin's family were riding out Hurricane Michael in their home, he went out and filmed the storm with his cellular phone under the shelter of his carport. While Kevin was out, a tree fell on his car. Despite the obvious dangers, Kevin and his family remained safe.

Ann Jones

On Wednesday the weather was so severe that Ann Jones, her husband, daughter-in-law and one grandchild sought safety in the hallway of their home. "Four trees fell on the house," Ann shared. One big pine tree knocked the front of the house off. The skylights were broken and rain poured into where they were staying. Then, a tree came through the living room wall. "We couldn't get out" she explained. "We were trapped." Ann remembered her neighbors had evacuated to a shelter before the storm. "During the eye we walked on the porch and our neighbor's house had been cut in two by a tree," she continued. "The second half of the storm was worse and I thought it would never stop," she added.

Georgeann Adkison

"On October 10th reality set in," Georgeann explained. The families staying together at the farm walked out during the eye of the storm and trees were down everywhere. Georgeann shared, "the oak trees near the front of the house had fallen on a dump truck." "The first half of the storm was the worst," she continued. "The doors and windows were trying to blow in." "The children stayed in the hallway, but everyone was calm," she added. According to Georgeann, there was water damage, but no structural damage to the house they were staying in. However, the barn had severe damage. "Afterwards some of us girls got a golf cart and went down to Highway 71," she continued. "We could hear people cutting a path down Highway 71 South." The ladies were without phones, cell phone reception, Internet, power, or communication. She remembered Florida Highway Patrol officers were everywhere. "My ex-husband had parked near Interstate 10 and with his dog had hiked several miles to check on us," she continued. "When the road was finally cleared, it looked like at least a hundred Florida Highway Patrol cars coming through."

Elizabeth Simpson

Elizabeth and John Simpson were home when Hurricane Michael came through Marianna. She remembered how her two daughters were calling to check on her regularly. The couple listened as trees fell on their home from north to south, and east to west. Then, the second floor wall of their office blew out.

Jay James

According to Jay, she and her daughter, Allison, were under a mattress when the storm arrived. "I was afraid the roof would come off my aunt's brick house," Jay shared. During the eye of the storm Jay and Allison walked around outside before quickly retreating for shelter. During the second half of the storm, Jay received a call from her husband, Robert, who told her a big tree had fallen through their home and he, his mother-in-law and the pets were in the den. Jay remembered hearing water.

Photos taken outside Jay James' home after the storm, where her husband, mother-in-law and pets were staying during the storm. Photos provided by Jay James.

Photos provided by Jay James.

Photos provided by Jay James.

Joan Schairer

Huge trees from neighboring properties that fell on Joan's home during
Hurricane Michael. Photo provided by Joan Schairer.

Joan remembered that around 1:30 p.m. the winds started
picking up and her electricity went out. It would only be an hour
later that she would begin feeling the first half of the storm. Joan
sought refuge in her master bedroom closet alone with her phone,
radio, secure items she wanted to save, and a pillow. She had left
the blinds open so she could see out and what she saw was
devastation. Trees were crashing, and the storm was wreaking
havoc on her neighborhood. "I heard something hit the roof and
all of a sudden my butt is wet," she explained. Joan couldn't
figure out why she was sitting in water. She dashed out and went
from room to room trying to figure out what was happening.
When she opened up the door between her kitchen and laundry
room, Joan discovered that a huge tree had sliced into her home.
"The rain was just pouring in," she continued. "All of a sudden I
hear the roof and the ceiling make this god-awful sound, and I

know its wind ripping down it," she continued. "And I really did, I said, 'Is this the end? Is this how it's going to end for me?'" she recalled with the upmost sincerity.

Top: Tree slicing through Joan's home between the mast and meter from the electrical box. Bottom: Trees from neighboring properties that fell on Joan's home. Photos provided by Joan Schairer.

When the eye came over her home, Joan went out to take photos and discovered there were three more trees in her home. She also discovered that the trusses in her home had been destroyed and the roof line of her house was wide open. Joan like many others went back inside during the eye of the storm and called her insurance company.

Photos provided by Joan Schairer.

Then, the eye picked up and I have never seen anything like that ever!" "I know that I was looking at a tornado" she continued. Joan went back to the internal closet for safety and listened at something hitting her home repeatedly. She would later learn that all the vinyl had been lifted up and was slapping back and forth.

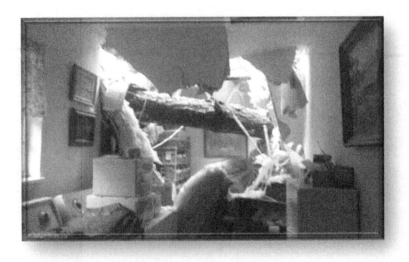

Photo provided by Joan Schairer.

Joan listened to what sounded to her like the roof being lifted up, and then, it settling back down. "By now, I'm stunned in the carnage of all the trees and all the damage, and it just keeps pounding and pounding and pounding," she shared. "Finally, it starts to ease off, so I get up, and look and my floor in the bedroom, the utility room, the kitchen, my closet and half-way into the dining area and living room is just sopping wet!" Joan had her photo albums stored in the living room, so she grabbed a tarp, which she had brought in while preparing, laid it down and tried to protect the items that could not be replaced. Joan explained how rain water spewed from all her light fixtures in her bedroom, utility room, kitchen and front bedroom on the south side of her home. "My utility room was toast!" When night fell on the City, Joan went to the front bedroom on the south side of her house, opened a window to feel the still strong winds. "I guess I laid down and went to sleep," she tried to remember.

Photo provided by Joan Schairer

Melissa Krebeck

On October 10th, 2018 Melissa was watching coverage of Hurricane Michael at home with her sons. She remembered that at about 11 a.m. her cable went out, leaving her without one source of information. However, she still had a weather radio and cellular service, so she did not feel isolated. "I wasn't overly concerned, but kept checking in with my mom, who lives in a little town called Irmo" she recalled. "At the beginning of the storm

45

we were watching the trees blow, and Evan, my youngest son made a comment that it looked like the trees were dancing," she shared. During the worst part of the storm, Melissa inflated their air mattresses. Then, Melissa, her two sons, two cats and dog sheltered the storm in this windowless hall sitting on the mattresses. Melissa felt that as long as broken glass did not hit them, they would be fine in their block home.

Photos provided by Melissa Krebeck.

46

SURVIVING HURRICANE MICHAEL: A COMMUNITY'S STORY OF DEVASTATION, SURVIVAL AND HOPE DURING RECOVERY

Photos provided by Melissa Krebeck.

When the first tree fell, Melissa could hear it brushing across the house before its landing, and she began to feel fearful. "Evan was really upset," she explained. "We sat around, holding hands, praying and trying to distract each other with stupid stuff until the worst of it had passed," Melissa shared. "When the center was here and it was an eerily calm, we went out onto the front porch," she continued. Melissa could see that the tree on the side of the house had wiped out power lines, which were on the ground. "I could see all my neighbors coming out of their houses, and we were all just looking around," she laughed. The trees in Melissa's front yard were down and the largest tree in the backyard had fallen. During the eye, two of Zachary's friends ran over to her house to check on them. She promptly sent them home to ride the storm out at their homes. Melissa was happy to see that her favorite oak tree was still standing, and was hoping her house would block the wind and the tree would survive. Unfortunately, the remainder of Melissa's trees fell after the eye passed over. "When everything was said and done, and you looked out, there was nothing," she explained. "My neighborhood was so pretty, so green and trees everywhere," she continued, "it was just ugly and it's still ugly!" "You can see the back of my house from three streets away, and there's no privacy," Melissa said sadly.

Royce Reagan

Royce Reagan shared how about 250 trees in their vicinity had fallen. Some of the trees were located on adjacent properties. This was the buffer and beautiful riverine environment Royce had once enjoyed. "When the storm was over, we were thankful that we only had to replace a couple of pieces of metal roofing, which had been installed about five or six years previously," he shared. Their A-frame house located near Chipola College had very steep

48

metal roofs. After a closer look around, Royce also discovered a little damage on their barn.

Michelle Borden

Michelle and her family were comfortable at home, when they noticed signs of the storm arriving about 1:30 p.m. "The power blinked three times and my boyfriend, who worked for an electric company at one time, knew that meant the power was going to go out," she explained. As they watched the wind and rain from their dining room window, the couple saw the first dead tree fall. Then, they noticed a tree in the back corner of the lot that was being twisted up before their eyes. "It looked like someone was giving the tree an Indian burn; all the bark was twisting," Michelle continued. That tree fell onto Michelle's home over her family room. "I thought 'we are in Marianna and these trees have been here forever and a day,'" she added. "That sucker was huge, and we watched the roof from the inside bounce up and down," Michelle continued. "Then the water gushed in." Michelle's brand new sofa that had been delivered only two weeks before the storm was ruined. The roof on the room bounced, but the tree, which also punctured the ceiling in the master bedroom, was holding the roof down and preventing it from blowing away. Michelle and her boyfriend began moving furnishings around and getting buckets for the water to prevent further damage.

That's when she decided the storm was probably not a category three.

Photo provided by Michelle Borden.

Michelle's boyfriend was from the northern United States and was fascinated by the storm. She explained how he was going outside periodically, and she was trying to explain that it wasn't safe. Prior to the storm her boyfriend had secured the children's outside playset with a hundred pound chain. The playset remained in place, but the bench at the corner of the house, Michelle watched fly away and destroy itself. "I told him even if it is a category three, things can go flying and you can be killed," she recalled pleading with him. He continued to go outside, but didn't leave the carport area. Meanwhile, both of the kids were in her daughter's bedroom playing.

It was at this point that Michelle decided that they needed to go to the bathroom for safety. "That's what you are taught in Florida growing up," Michelle explained. "You go to an interior bathroom, where there are no windows and that was the only one for us," she continued. Michelle gathered the children's beanbags, pillows and blankets. Then, she took the children to the bathroom, where they were happily playing on their tablets. "I put my purse on the counter, and was thinking what else do I need to have in here in case this is the last place we need to be," she recalled. Then, Michelle went after one of the children's mattresses to place over them.

The children's bedrooms where they were playing. Photos provided by Michelle Borden.

Along the way she noticed her boyfriend standing at the window watching the storm. "I said this is the worst place for you to be, and I'm staying away from you," she added. "When you die, I don't want to watch it happen." Then, she returned to the bathroom to stay with the children. Michelle remembered that suddenly, her boyfriend came around the corner and yelled "get out of the bathroom! Get the kids out of the bathroom!" She didn't question him and told the kids to quickly leave the room. Along the way her son dropped his tablet. Michelle stopped to get the tablet and two trees came into the room at the same time.

"If you look at the photograph carefully, there is a triangle and we probably would have been hurt, but okay," she explained. Michelle probably stood more of an opportunity for injury protecting her children against the trees. It took Michelle a minute to make sure nothing else would fall, while she was leaving. Once Michelle was sure she wouldn't be trapped, she came out to find her family in tears. Michelle's little girl thought she was dead. While she suffered scratches, cuts and bruises from the trees falling into the room, Michelle was on an adrenaline rush and did not experience any pain until the following day.

Michelle told her boyfriend to go to the family room area, because there were no trees remaining on that side of the house. He took the children to the corner of the room. That's when Michelle realized that she was in her pajamas and didn't have any shoes on. She quickly grabbed her sneakers and put them on. In the same room, there were four small windows near where she was sitting. "While I was sitting there, the top right window exploded" she shared. "It was like a gunshot and glass was everywhere."

The family sat and cuddled closely together by the fireplace surrounded by furniture, while she began to watch the storm on her phone. "I realized we were on the edge of the eye wall, and started telling my boyfriend 'the eye wall is going to get worse before it gets better,'" she explained, "'and then it's going to be nothing for about half an hour.'" The couple began evaluating whether anything else could possibly fall on them. The only tree they noticed was at a neighbor's house. They would later learn that tree had fallen on the same neighbor's home.

Photos provided by Michelle Borden.

"Ironically, the laundry room was beside the family room, and I had just done laundry," she added, "but the laundry basket was full of only my clothes". She had already folded and put the children's clothes away. This would leave her with one outfit for her son and one dress for her daughter. The clothes Michelle had were workout clothes that she had hung to dry in the laundry room "I wore compression pants for two days," she shared. The next weekend they would find a few more clothes in the dryer that they didn't think of during the trauma of the storm.

Photos provided by Michelle Borden.

During the eye of the storm the family walked out and a neighbor across the street, Jean Wise, took them in. Jean also took in a couple of other families nearby, including an elderly lady who could not care for herself. Jean and her son had one tree to fall on their house, but they were able to catch most of the water in a bucket. While Michelle was getting the kids settled at the Wise's home, her boyfriend went back to grab some things and she called her insurance company. Meanwhile, her boyfriend filled a duffel bag and laundry basket with all the food he could carry. While he was at her home, he had to stop and rest for a few minutes. "I started flipping out thinking 'where are you? Why aren't you back here?'" she shared. "It's going to start again soon and it's going to be another eye wall," she recalled panicking. When he did arrive just as the eye wall was coming back to them, she remembered him saying "I don't know what your problem is - it's nice and quiet!" Michelle remembered the second half of the storm to be shorter than the first half. "There was a lot more wind and rain, but less stuff flying," she shared.

Paula Livergood

During the storm Paula and her children could hear the trees cracking and falling. "We felt, it when they hit the house," she shared. Paula recalled the electrical power going out during the first hour. Then, they watched their wood privacy fence blow away. Paula remembered to pass the time they counted as they heard trees falling, until they lost count.

When they had determined the storm had calmed, Paula was able to go out the back door during the eye of the storm. They could only go out a short distance out the side door, because it was blocked by fallen trees. While they were outside, it was raining, but the wind wasn't as heavy. "Then, we could hear what sounded like a tornado or two," she continued. They didn't stay outside long, because the wind and sound continued to pick up. The family retreated upstairs to the hallway. "Our dog wouldn't leave our side," Paula added.

The second half of the storm was "nerve racking" Paula shared. "It seemed like it lasted forever." Water came into their house through side and front doors during the hurricane. Water also came down on them in the upstairs hallway during the storm. Paula wanted to stay in touch with her father who lives near the downtown area. She knew his small home was surrounded by trees. However, her cellular service was touch and go. She was able to receive calls from a couple of her neighbors. One family told Paula that they were under their table because trees had gone through their windows and into their roof. It would be a couple of days before they could get to one another. Meanwhile, Paula's mother rode out the storm in the basement, where the sounds where muffled. She later reported enjoying the sounds.

Ronnie Keel

As the weather deteriorated Ronnie began watching a Sugar Hackberry Tree in his front yard. The more the wind increased, the more the tree leaned further and further down. Ronnie decided the tree was probably going to blow over and was aimed at his wife's car. "I went out and moved her car across the street," he explained. Ronnie decided to move the truck too, so it wouldn't be blocked by a fallen tree. When he was out moving his truck, he noticed his neighbor, James Lash, had decided that it might be a good idea to follow suit. "While we were both out in the yard, the first one of the big oak trees fell across his house," Ronnie shared. "So, I ran over to help him, but the tree had squished his house sideways enough that he couldn't open the door," he continued. The men had to break into the house, because James' wife, Catherine, was in the front, northwest bedroom. "That's where the tree had fell, and had the ceiling mashed down to about shoulder height," Ronnie continued. Catherine was in a hospital bed and unable to get up. "While we were checking on her, the second one of those big oak trees fell across his house," Ronnie explained. The men began moving Catherine to the kitchen. That's when a third oak tree fell across James' house. "By this time, it has got it pretty well mashed flat,"

Ronnie explained. While the ceiling was almost like normal in the kitchen, the bedrooms couldn't be entered, because they were so low to the floor. The room where Catherine had been, the third tree had flattened too low to enter. He left them in the kitchen to ride out the storm.

Ronnie decided to return home. During the time he had been at James' house, the Sugar Hackberry Tree had fallen. So, he had to climb over the tree to go home. "I just sat it out, and finally the eye came over," he explained, "and I was worried about the barn, and the chickens and all this kinda stuff." Ronnie has a farm south of town. "I thought maybe I should get out and check on those things," he shared. "Well, heck, I couldn't get out to the street, much less get the car down the street," he continued. It would be two days before they could move a vehicle down the street. So, Ronnie waited out the storm at home. "The first part was probably the worst, because all the trees had blown down by the time the second part got there," he described. "I had a metal cover over the top of the chimney to keep it from raining down the chimney that blew off down the roof and knocked half a dozen holes the size of your fist and smaller in the roof," he shared. He also lost some of the siding and a portion of the soffit.

James Lash

During the first part of the storm James saw his neighbor Ronnie Keel outside, and went to move his vehicle. "The first tree fell and hit her bedroom, but didn't completely collapse it," he explained. James and the two Ronnies moved Catherine with a hoist to the wheelchair, and then to the kitchen. Afterwards James went back to get the mattress off Catherine's hospital bed and put it down in front of the sink. "I knew she wouldn't be able to sit in that wheelchair forever," he explained. James moved her to the mattress in front of the sink. "By that time the next two trees hit and collapsed the living room and the back bedroom completely," James continued. James found himself trapped in one room with Catherine and Ronnie Lollie. His bedroom was crushed to only two feet tall. "Nothing could be saved from that room," he shared. "If we had been in that room, we wouldn't be sitting here and talking today."

James Lash in front of his house that was demolished by Hurricane Michael.
Photos provided by Debbie Lollie.

Two days later, when his grandchildren brought the firemen to rescue them, the door had to be kicked down. James' great granddaughter gathered up her FFA friends and together they cut a path through the debris. "They knocked on the door about 2 a.m.," he shared. "There was an ambulance and a fire truck sitting down on South Street," he continued. "They carried her to Chipley, because that was the only place receiving," he added. The following morning after the road was cleared where he could drive out, James went to stay with Catherine in Chipley and Ronnie Lollie went to check on his home.

James Lash following the rescue workers who were taking his wife, Catherine to the hospital in the middle of the night. Photo provided by Debbie Lollie.

Ronstance Pittman

Ronstance recalled Hurricane Michael being quite scary. "I sent my daughter to the hallway bathroom, and my daughter was praying," she expressed. "My husband was standing at the door holding the door open and I was like 'Close the Door!'" Ronstance's mother stood at the back door and watched the neighbor's tree as it was uprooted. "It was like a ghost was picking it up," she explained. "It was like the longest moment, where you are just terrified."

During the eye, they were able to go out and the carport had fallen on Roger's car. It would take a crane to move it weeks later. The family lost shingles from their home and their swimming pool was full of debris. Ronstance explained, "the wind was so strong that when it was raining, water came through the windows."

Shaleigh described how the night after Hurricane Michael there "was hot water, no lights, and sadly, no phone service." "We started looking around and it was like a war had happened or like bombs had gone off," Ronstance added.

Carmen Smith

Carmen Smith remembered sitting at her parent's home in Tallahassee and enjoying the breeze, while having no idea what was to come. After the storm passed through, a neighbor texted Carmen wanting to know when she was going to return to see her home. Where Carmen's family had been staying in Tallahassee, the storm was not bad, but they did experience loss of power. The debris that she remembered seeing when she was leaving Tallahassee was nothing compared to what she saw entering Gadsden County.

Kenny Griffin

Kenny Griffin shared how his family lived just southwest of Marianna, which was on the outside edge of the storm's eye. Being on the eye-wall edge meant the storm was severe for a long period of time without a break. He had water pouring into his

home, because the storm lifted up his roof. "I looked up and
water was pouring down the pull chain of the ceiling fan like a
water hose," Kenny continued. He had one tree fall on his house,
but it didn't do much damage. "A lot depended on the angle the
house was sitting and the direction of the wind," he explained.

Kenny shared how the wind blew down two large barns,
flipped a big, heavy corrugated building upside down, and blew
down a countless amount of fencing on his farm. Kenny lost five
head of livestock. Although he doesn't know what happened to
his cows, Kenny speculates some may have been injured by flying
debris, and some may have eaten the leaves of wild cherry trees,
which are highly toxic to cattle.

During the storm a big 24 foot piece of metal had pulled away
from his home and fallen behind the house instead of blowing
over. The wind was picking up the piece of metal and slamming
it up against the house during the storm. Thinking it would bust
out the back windows, he decided to leave the house on the
southern side, where the wind wasn't as bad. As he walked
around the building, a gust blew him down to the ground. "It was
good because it made me think grabbing the tin wasn't a good
idea." So, Kenny began stomping on the tin. He grabbed the
chain attached to his grandchildren's wooden outdoor play set,
and it collapsed onto the tin. "By that time I heard a tree crack, I
said 'I've got to get out of here!'"

Inside his French doors were blowing back and forth. Kenny
placed a recliner, a dresser and other furniture against the doors
to keep them from blowing open. Kenny shared that he knew of
at least three homes where the French doors blew in. "We took

ours out immediately after the storm!" Kenny's neighbors had a Florida room. When she opened the door to step into the room, the glass exploded cutting her face.

"The first morning when I checked, the gate and post were out in the road," Kenny explained. He went on to share how he noticed that on the east side of Jackson County the trees were laying down in one direction, but on the west side of town it was another.

Joshua Glass

Nineteen year old Joshua Glass worked as a Certified Nursing Assistant for Signature Healthcare at the Courtyard just east of town. While Hurricane Michael was coming through Marianna, Joshua was called in for emergency duty. He left his home and began heading toward the east side of town, making his way to work. As he approached where Noland Street intersects Lafayette Street, the weather was too strong for him to go any further. Joshua saw a storm chaser traveling east in a van. He left his vehicle and the storm chaser took him to work, where he would stay for days.

The people in Marianna were caught off guard by the power of Hurricane Michael. They were forced to make decisions they never imagined they would face. Yet, they came together to protect themselves, their families and their neighbors. This would be the first of many times in the year ahead that neighbors would help neighbors.

Chapter Four

First Responders Riding Out the Storm

Photo provided by Debbie Lash Lollie.

O n October 10th, City Manager Jim Dean was at work. At lunch he began to notice debris blowing, so he went home to ride out the storm with his wife. Jim remembered not going out during the eye of the storm. Joe Richey, Public Works Director was at his home, only a couple of blocks from City Hall and Doug Glass, Natural Gas Supervisor was home, as well. However, natural gas employees were stationed and ready to act. Rick Harrell, Water and Wastewater Supervisor, was at the Wastewater Treatment Plant with six employees stationed for action. During the eye of Hurricane Michael, Rick and his staff walked around to assess damage.

Marianna Fire Department checking things out during the eye of Hurricane Michael. Photo provided by Police Chief Hayes Baggett.

Marianna Fire Department

Captain Watson shared how his family was scattered. His wife worked the night before the storm and went home to be joined by Clint's mother and step-father. Clint's son lives at Silver Lake in a mobile home, but came into town and sheltered at a church on Kelson Avenue. Clint was with his supervisor, and his father, who works for the Jackson County Sheriff's Department, at the Emergency Operations Center. They had arrived during the early evening hours on Tuesday. Clint was able to text back

64

and forth with his family throughout the storm to make sure everyone was okay.

Dispatch was at the Emergency Operations Center and we were listening to 911 calls coming in. No one could respond during the storm to provide help. "That was a nightmare!" According to Clint, calls ranged from being hurt to being trapped. "Dispatch just told them 'I'm sorry we can't get out to help you,'" he continued, "'you'll have to wait until we can.'" "It was tough just to listen to it!" Clint added.

Clint Watson walking down the street after some of the fallen trees had been removed. Photo provided by Clint Watson.

Clint and others watched the roof at Jackson County Road and Bridge Building be blown off and hit the Emergency Operations Building they were in. There were only a few medical professionals at the Emergency Operations Center, so when people would step outside, Clint was constantly trying to keep them inside where it was safe. It was important, because there was no place to take anyone who got hurt. "There was a group of people who lived down the road, whose trailer was destroyed," Clint added. "They came up with no place to go, so we had to let them in the Emergency Operations Center."

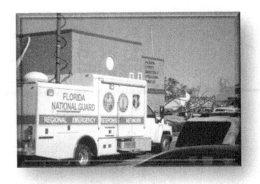

The Emergency Operations Center (EOC). Photos provided by Scott Hagan.

The remains of the Jackson County Road and Bridge Facility after Hurricane Michael. Photo provided by Rhonda Dykes.

Photo provided by Scott Hagan.

More than half of the Marianna Fire Department were on duty at the City Hall Fire Station, and communicating back and forth with reports to Clint and his supervisor. "The doors at City Hall flew open repeatedly, and they kept having to hold the doors closed," Clint shared. "They tied them up with something." The Police Chief would later explain the doors were tied with extension cords. "The window upstairs was blown out and my supervisor's office was flooded," Clint continued, "and they moved all his stuff back away from the wall because the rain was just pouring in from there."

Marianna Police Department

Police Chief Hayes Baggett explained that the night of the storm the Marianna Police Department phone lines were out. "We had one back up line and that was a blessing," Chief Baggett shared. "Officer Triston Arroyo had a tree on his house, and he couldn't go home," he continued. "We didn't think it would be this bad," Becky Partin, Chief Baggett's Administrative Assistant, expressed in shock, "it never had before." Chief Baggett recalled "the sign on the door of City Hall stated 'we will be open October 11th'".

Before the storm Hayes and his staff had boarded up their storefront window, and fueled their City police cars. "We didn't bring everyone in," he shared. With a staff of one dispatcher, six officers, four investigators, an administrative assistant, his wife Amber, and their dogs, Chief Baggett and his dedicated team rode the storm out at the Marianna Police Station. "At first we saw light poles falling like dominoes and a stop sign was spinning" Lieutenant Stroud reported. "At 11:45 a.m. the power went out," Chief Baggett continued. "I was worried about family," Becky shared. Despite their personal concerns the Marianna Police Department continued their dedication to the City of Marianna. "It didn't look untenable at the door," shared Lieutenant Stroud, who had been to the dentist to have his wisdom teeth cut out the day before the storm.

Lieutenant Stroud had sent his family to Bascom to shelter during the storm, which turned out to be a good move since their home was totally destroyed. During the eye of the storm, the on duty police department ventured out and took photos of the firefighters eager to get started with the cleanup.

Storm damaged flags flying over the Marianna Post Office. Photo taken by Police Chief Baggett following Hurricane Michael.

Photos taken immediately after the storm. Photos provided by Police Chief
Hayes Baggett.

Public Works

The shelter Sam Everett stayed at would not allow anyone to
go outside and look around. Just a few minutes after the eye of

the storm started passing over the shelter, a Fire Rescue Team had learned of a family trapped in their home in Sneads. The Team was trying to figure out how to rescue them. "When they found out that I worked for the City of Marianna, they said we need you to help navigate," Sam shared.

Sam and Charlie went out during the second half of the storm. First, they went south on Caverns Road toward downtown Marianna, navigating around fallen trees and power lines and at times driving on the steep road edge. They were able to go as far as Yancey Bridge at the Chipola River. There they saw that Caverns Road and River Forest Road were just covered with trees. "We could see a long line of police lights in the distance by Chipola College," Sam continued. "When we saw we couldn't get through, we were going to try to stop and work." "We couldn't, so we turned and went back down Caverns Road," he explained. "Then we turned . . . [north] . . . on Old US Road thinking we might be able to go around the Greenwood way," Sam recalled.

Toppled train at the M.E.R.E. Complex. **Above:** photo provided by Amber Baggett. **Left:** photo provided by Rhonda Dykes.

Top: Historic Marianna High School on Daniels Street with trees blocking the roadway.

Middle: Photo of what most streets looked like in Marianna.

Bottom: Chipola College Sign on Kelson Avenue.

Photos provided by Scott Hagan

The men didn't make it very far, because trees were down everywhere. So, they turned around with the rescue workers

72

following in a pickup truck. Whenever they arrived at Caverns Road, Sam and Charlie turned east and drove by the shelter they had been staying at making their way towards Highway 71. About a quarter of a mile east of Marianna High School on the north side of Caverns Road is the Marianna Educational Recreational Expo (M.E.RE.) Complex. When Sam and Charlie were near the M.E.R.E. Complex, they saw the train turned over. "The wind was rocking us a little bit and we see lines all over the road," Sam continued. "I was calling on the name of Jesus, because who else could help?" When they arrived at Highway 71, they turned south, but again didn't make it far. "Trees were just all across the road," Sam recalled. So, the men turned around to go north toward Greenwood. "We got as far as Fire and Rescue, and trees were just all over the road." "We couldn't .get them out, so we said 'maybe we need to go back to where those State Troopers were at," Sam explained "with other people, maybe we could at least get one of those roads opened".

By that time Zach and Lee Hunter, brothers who work in Public Works, had made it to Jefferson Street. Sam continued, "we start trying to come up with a plan, because they have their family out at the Gas Division," which is located on the north side of town at the Marianna Municipal Airport. Joe Richey, Public Works Director had left the front-end loader at City Hall and the men were trying to get to it, so they could begin clearing the streets. "The storm is still going on," Sam continued.

Gulf Coast Utility Contractors (GCUC) had been working with Chipola College, the City of Marianna and David H. Melvin, Incorporated on a stormwater pond for the college. Sam and the other men learned that GCUC had left a piece of heavy equipment at the job site. "Whenever we got over there, they didn't have anything that we could use," Sam explained. "So we walked all the way to College Street and one of the guys said 'we have a backhoe at the gas department,'" he shared. So, during the second half of Hurricane Michael coming through Marianna, the men maneuvered their way back around. These men were working on adrenaline in some of the most dangerous conditions ever seen in the area.

Marianna Health and Rehab

While Melinda Gay's family was at home riding out the storm, she and approximately 150 others with their families sheltered inside the Marianna Health and Rehab facility. "We really didn't have time to worry about what was going on outside, because we were trying to focus on keeping the residents and children calm," she explained. Melinda takes dedication to the facility to a high level. She ensured there was popcorn, movies, and snow cones. "The power went out around 1 p.m. and we lost water about 3 p.m.," she shared. During the eye of the storm, staff went out to get more supplies. While they didn't have time to focus on the storm, she remembered watching their three awnings blow away. Families wanted to be with their loved ones.

"Trees dropped in front of the building, but we didn't know," she added. They became aware of roof damage when her staff discovered four different spots that were leaking. Melinda's team at Marianna Health and Rehab used garbage cans and linen barrels to catch the rain fall, which later proved helpful in flushing toilets. After the storm was over, they tied the doors shut.

Recreation Department

Clay Wells shared how his mother, next door neighbor and Crystle's aunt and cousins came over, because their home had a basement. Clay wasn't overly concerned about the storm until trees started falling around the house. After the storm was over, he discovered that there were two holes in their roof, all the shingles had been blown off, and there were two broken windows. His yard was full of trees, downed fences and debris. Yet, Clay was thankful that everyone had survived safely.

Florida Public Utilities

Mason Brock watched the news until the stations went off the air. Then, he went under the porch and watched trees breaking on buildings. During the eye of the storm, Mason walked around and assessed the damage. Then, the back side of the storm came through. Mason was able to communicate with his family with cellular service until midnight. During this time he started making calls to the company.

Jackson Hospital

Emergency entrance to Jackson Hospital after Hurricane Michael. Photo provided by Scott Hagan.

Kevin Daniel, Engineering Director for Jackson Hospital explained how patients were moved into crowded corridors for safety. The primary objective was to keep them away from the windows. "While Jackson Hospital did not sustain damage, the roof on the Hudnall Building peeled back and both floors were flooded," Kevin continued. "There was some water in the hospital that came in through vents and windows, but we were very fortunate that we didn't sustain structural damage." There were fences, trees and cars in the parking lot damaged, but the main issue for the hospital was water in the building. "Some of the electronic equipment was damaged too, but it was repaired," Kevin stated.

Building Official

"It was unbelievable," shared Building Official Jimmy Grant. "I looked at it thinking 'things like that don't happen here,'" he added. Jimmy and his wife, Janet, watched as a big oak tree fell through his office. The couple had three trees on the house, three on the barn/office area and they lost more than 60 trees on their five acre parcel. "My wife was scared to death," Jimmy explained. The couple walked around outside during the eye of the storm and were greeted by a neighbor who said "sure am glad it's over". It wasn't over though. However, Jimmy shared that the back part of the storm didn't seem as bad, which might have been because all of his trees were down. "Even though I had a mess, I was luckier than the rest."

City Commissioner Rico Williams

"During the storm we didn't have a break" Commissioner Williams shared. His parent's house had been in the path of the intense side of the eye wall. He explained how he saw trees falling everywhere and it seemed like it would never end. Commissioner Williams' father and thirteen year-old son, Corey, went to the truck, so they could see the storm. "They pulled up just a little bit and a tree fell right by the truck," he continued. "We had five or six vehicles outside and the Lord laid the trees right in between them!" "It was just amazing with all the damage and devastation that we had no major catastrophes," Commissioner Williams added.

Jackson County Administrator

The storm came while Wilanne and her family were at her in-law's house. "It was terrifying!" "We put the kids in the laundry room and leaned an air mattress over them," Wilanne explained. "At one point I asked Ryan ... [her husband] ... to come in and pray for us, because when I looked out the window there were huge trees toppling." Wilanne remembered holding her baby and having her two other small children beside her wondering "if something happens, how I am going to gather them all up together." "At the same time I was thinking about what this meant for the County, but to be honest I still did not have a comprehension of what we were about to face," Wilanne explained.

Their phones stopped working until sometime in the night following the storm. "I couldn't find out anything, or how anyone was," she continued. "That's when we realized that we were completely blocked in." "As silly as it sounds, I thought we were the only ones blocked in," she clarified because of the isolation she was experiencing. "I felt like everyone would wonder where I was and I was very upset," she clarified. Her father-in-law, husband and another man went out right away making a path with their tractors. As soon as they were able to get a path cleared, Ryan drove her and the baby to the Emergency Operations Center.

Jackson County Sheriff's Office

Martin Basford patrolled until the weather was too difficult to drive in, and then, he joined his family at the Chipola College Public Service Building. He watched from the west side of the building as all the pine trees near the adjacent homes broke off simultaneously. He saw the Chipola College stormwater metal culvert,that weighed about 500 pounds, blow away from the pond to Long House Court. "I tried to stay calm and hide my anxiety from my family," he shared.

Michael Mears was at work when the storm hit. "It was like a four to five hour long tornado that just would not end," he shared. "It was just very, very strong and I've never seen anything like it in my life!"

He shared how he was on patrol when Hurricane Michael came through Jackson County. "I remember getting on the radio and telling everyone to seek shelter," he continued. "I called a friend of mine and literally told him to open the door and get out of the way." Mike was trapped inside his friend's house for several hours. Together they watched the pine trees beside the house as they were snapped off about ten feet off the ground. "It was almost like a giant weed-eater was eating everything up" Mike added. "My buddy, who was in the navy, said it reminded him of Afghanistan, like a war zone without the smoke!" Mike explained how it seemed like time stood still and he lost track of time.

No one was prepared for Hurricane Michael. In retrospect one wonders if total preparation was even possible. Yet, during the storm, they were already stepping up to face fears they had never imagined. Marianna leaders and first responders were already putting aside their own concerns to help others. Some would not be able to check on their homes for days to come. Much like the citizens riding out the storm at home, these community leaders would find their comfort in God and helping others.

PART III

What Now?

Marianna was devastated by Hurricane Michael. Residents, first responders and community leaders were trapped by fallen trees on every road in town. The trees covered the roads to the point of locals not knowing where the roads were located. People were hurt and sick, but first responders were unable to make a difference until the roadways were cleared. The outside world was unable to enter, and the inside City was unable to connect.

Despite these setbacks, a tenacious community would pull together to help one another. Neighbors helped neighbors cut trees from the roads to clear paths. People shared resources until and after others came from outside the community to provide help.

If the community had not worked together, initial response times would have taken longer. Getting help meant being the help needed.

Above: Florida Wildlife Commission arriving after Hurricane Michael. Photo provided by Scott Hagan. **Left**: Temporary sleeping quarters in the Fire Bay for first responders helping the City. Photo provided by Kelsey Escoriaza. **Below**: Linemen arrive to help restore power. Photo provided by Lori Nable.

Top: Debris hauling trucks staged at the M.E.R.E. Complex.

Middle: Staging area with showers and Air Conditioned sleeping areas for workers.

Bottom: Mormons, who came to assist, camping in tents at Chipola College. Photos provided by Rhonda Dykes.

Chapter Five

Are We Trapped?

The first step to responding to a devastating hurricane is to evaluate where you are and where you want to be. Many residents were emotionally traumatized simply from riding out the storm. Others would find themselves in distress as they viewed the devastation around them. However, being in shock doesn't imply paralysis. Emotional consternation might provide the mental protection for people to go the extra mile, despite their own needs. It might provide people the will to keep moving forward despite despair lurking around every corner. Emotional trauma might be the cushion people need to work their way back to what they loved before Hurricane

Michael. It might be what keeps people in check with what is most important in the world and in their own lives.

Photos provided by Lori Nable.

Photos provided by Scott Hagan.

Photos provided by Scott Hagan.

Photos provided by Scott Hagan.

Jay James

Jay's husband Bobby explained that the roof on their home was compromised. Their kitchen, living room, front bedroom and bathroom were destroyed. Rain had been pouring into Jay's once childhood home. Their sunken den was flooded with at least a couple of inches of water and the electricity was out.

Jay's potbellied pig, Buttercup, was outside in their gazebo. Jay's husband, Bobby tried to secure the outside and pig. Buttercup was on her mind, but at that time there was nothing they could do other than secure the pig as best as possible and ensure there was ample food and water. She thought about how Buttercup barked like a dog and was an escape artist. In fact, Jay remembered how one night before the storm, Buttercup had broken out and was under the neighbor's window barking.

The storm had ripped off the carport and blocked Jay's car. Allison's car had damage too. Jay's aunt had faired much better, losing only a few shingles, wooden privacy fence around her pool and a few fallen trees. So, Bobby and his mother took her car to Jay's aunt's house to join the family. Bobby also brought their dog.

On Saturday the family would visit a friend in DeFuniak Springs to take showers and pickup groceries. The same day Jay called her insurance company. She remembered taking food out of the freezer and grilling it.

Jay's second home and all their clothes were destroyed. Jay and Bobby worked with ALE Solutions and their insurance company to find a place to stay. The family had to go to Tallahassee, which is approximately 70 miles east and in a different time zone. Jay's mother-in-law couldn't get through to her house at that time, so she went with them to Tallahassee.

Jay recalled that when the family arrived at the Hampton Inn on Appalachee Parkway, the girl at the counter spent all afternoon trying to help them. Before it was over Jay and her family would load up and go to the new Hampton Inn by Florida State University. The first hotel had been dog friendly, but the second hotel wouldn't allow their dog. The clerk at the counter called the general manager, who would only agree for their dog to stay two days. So, Jay would take their dog back to her aunt's home and stay the night.

The following morning the girl from the hotel called back and had found them a place with a suite that included a kitchen, bedroom and bathroom. Jay returned with the dog. Free breakfast and dinner was an additional blessing. However, commuting from Tallahassee to work every day required her to leave before breakfast and return after dinner. Jay's mother-in-law stayed with the dog, while Allison took one car and commuted to Chipola College for classes. Jay and Bobby took the other car and commuted to work.

The first few days they traveled back and forth to feed Buttercup. Then, one day when they drove out to meet the adjuster, there were three Emergency Medical Technician's doing well-checks. One offered to take Buttercup to live on his farm in Quincy. With few better options, Jay allowed Buttercup to go live on the farm.

The hotel Jay and her family were staying in cost them $1400 a week plus fuel and food. Their coverage only allowed $15,400 total. So, they needed a place to stay that was less expensive and didn't require a commute.

Photo provided by Kay Dennis.

Photos provided by Kay Dennis.

Joan Schairer

The next morning Joan woke up and found she still had running water from the City of Marianna. After washing off, she walked around to survey the damage. That is when Joan discovered that she had another tree in her house. "That fourth tree plugged the hole and that is why the roof settled down," she explained. "The wind couldn't get into it as strongly as it had when it was gaping open." The garage had nine trusses destroyed. Her roof had multiple holes throughout its entirety. "Even when they tried to blue tarp it, they didn't find them all" she added referring to the holes in the roof. "The tarps did not work," Joan shared with exasperation. Without trusses the rain would sheet flow down the seams of the tarp into her home.

Photo provided by Joan Schairer.

"When I crawled out Thursday morning, we didn't have cell service," she continued. Joan had been texting her neighbors during the storm. She decided to walk down and check on them. Together they sat outside and enjoyed each other's company in the aftermath of what Joan referred to as "the monster". "All of a

91

sudden we had cell service and we all made calls to family," she explained. Joan knew how difficult it must be for her sons to wonder about her welfare. She let her sons, and ex-husband know that she had survived. Though they wanted to come and help her, she had to explain that it was impossible, because she was trapped.

Fourth Street in front of Joan's home. Photo provided by Joan Schairer.

Joan's vehicle was un-drivable. She nicknamed it "The blue whale" after the storm, because it was stationary in her driveway from October 12th until sometime in January. "The trees in the road were unbelievable" Joan explained. "They were bent over but they were still huge eighty feet tall pine trees that had just been snapped and dumped in the street." Joan was on the outskirts of Hurricane Camille when she lived in Fort Walton Beach, but she had never been in the eye before. She had seen damage in other hurricanes, but nothing like what was experienced in Marianna and Mexico Beach with Hurricane Michael. "It was beyond my wildest imagination, what we incurred and the wrath that we incurred from it."

Above: Joan's vehicle that was in the garage during Hurricane Michael, aka "The Blue Whale". Photo provided by Joan Schairer.

While Joan's grill was destroyed in the garage, she had some supplies and snacks. "The stuff I was going to use to cook with, I couldn't get to," she explained. "I couldn't heat anything." "I couldn't even heat coffee." Her neighbor didn't have as much damage, but had a grill. So, they pooled resources for survival, which created a lasting bond between them.

"My neighbors and I could see up the hill within the City limits a bobcat and someone with a gas saw working their way down the hill on Friday after the storm," Joan explained. "Our driveways are probably one hundred feet apart and Dr. Cook's son had taken his chainsaw and gotten down as far as he could, which included my next door neighbor's driveway," she explained. "He came up to me apologizing and said 'Joan I can't get into that because you've got way too many trees for what power I've got.'" Joan and her neighbors continued to watch as the bobcat reached about half-way down the street to their location. At noon the workers quit working and left. Although Joan chased them on foot, she failed to catch the workers and they didn't return. "So, I called Commissioner Lockey and said I have some problems here with some trees," she explained. Commissioner Chuck Lockey and his wife, Susan, had sustained incomprehensible damage at their recently remodeled home just a few blocks away. "He said 'Joan, we don't take trees,'" she recalled laughing. "I said 'no, I'm not talking about that,'" she explained. "I said 'whoever has been clearing the road has left and we have twenty foot tall piles of trees." "He said 'let me find Howard'" she continued. Commissioner Lockey was referring to former Commissioner Howard Glass, who works as a Supervisor at Jackson County Road and Bridge. Before long Joan saw a Jackson County Truck coming through on Fourth Street. "He said 'my gosh, it took me forever for me to get here!'" she shared. "He came up to me and said 'We've been working . . . [County Road] . . . 162, and nothing looks as bad as what you guys have gotten!'" Howard brought in a couple of guys with heavy equipment and chainsaws, and before dark they had cleared a path through that one hundred feet or so, that would connect Joan and her neighbors to partially cleared roadways. This allowed her neighbors, who had three children, to come and go. "I was extremely worried about them, but the County came through big time!"

Joan's ex-husband and his wife were waiting for the crew to clear the path. About thirty minutes behind them was one of Joan's sons. Joan's family was tremendous help and she was very grateful for their assistance. Together they decided to go over and check out Joan's mom's home. Joan thought the garage door looked like a shelf. There was also a busted out window. "And my mom's old blazer did not have one scratch on it," Joan shared laughing. "I thought 'why didn't I park my truck that was seven years younger here.'" Joan's mom's house needed a new roof, window and garage door. Joan shared that the garage door and window were installed in January. "A volunteer group helped my son and ex-husband get the garage door out, beat it straight again, and then, they shoved it up in to secure the house," she added. "Then, we used blue canvas tarps, cut it up, and used gorilla duct tape, best stuff ever made, around that window, because it was raining hard after that, and would have soaked that house," she described. Joan's ex-husband and his wife spent the night there, and her son went with her back to what was left of her house. All Joan had was a couch and a bed to sleep on. "Hot, my God, it was terribly hot!"

The following day the only family with Joan was her son, Jeff. Jeff insisted that she get some cooking capabilities. So, the two of them went to the south side Walmart in Dothan to eat, and buy a gas grill. Joan's neighbor bought a generator. He let Joan hook up to his generator via an extension cord. This allowed her to run a couple of fans, a floor light and charge her phone. They pooled their money for gas. Jeff stayed about a week. "During that time the insurance adjuster showed and the insurance company sent a roofer out of Jacksonville that had a crane to get the trees out of the house and to tarp it," she explained.

"So, life went on and kinda forgot about us," she continued "and when I say us, I'm referring to the area in general." "I called that number that you are supposed to be able to call when you need help or help line, and got nothing" she explained. Joan called multiple times a day and entered her zip code and was unable to attain any help. "I did it for a whole week just to see what would happen, and sometimes I would do it twice a day, because I was bored and didn't have anything else to do."

Finally, Joan put a note on Facebook, asking about food and showers. By this time her son was gone. She did receive a response about the Red Cross being at Marianna High School, but moving out the next day. There were showers, washing machines and dryers for public use. While Joan's son had been in town, they had gone over to Milton, and her ex-husband had treated them to showers, steak dinners and other niceties. Her ex-husband's wife took all of Joan's dirty clothes and washed them. "She even took the towels I had used to soak up the nastiness that was coming in and washed, dried and folded them up," Joan shared. "She cleaned up the glass in the garage at mom's house," Joan added. Joan was thankful for them. A group from the Mobile area tarped the houses in her mom's subdivision, because they knew it was a seniors' subdivision.

Melissa Krebeck

The day after the storm Melissa and her sons walked up to Saint Lukes Episcopal Church and First Presbyterian to see if there was any storm damage. "It took a lot just to get out of our neighborhood, because the trees were so bad," she shared. Melissa and her boys climbed over trees to find the churches. "I think that was a good thing for the boys, because I think they realized it was going to be a while before we had things back." Meanwhile, her neighbors were coming together with chainsaws trying to cleanup.

Photos taken on October 11, 2018 and provided by Melissa Krebeck.

Melissa's mom was upset and worried. It would only be two days after the storm that she would come into town with food and supplies. "I'm still eating from the cans of tuna she brought," Melissa said jokingly. Her family was able to use the water in the barrel to flush the toilet and they had bottled water for drinking. Although she didn't have a generator, they were accustomed to the weather from camping and the heat was not as hard on them. She set up her camp stove and table outside. "We just lived outside," she continued. "We'd go in at night and sleep with our battery operated fans and it wasn't horrible." In fact, Melissa and her boys spent family time together reading books and playing games. Although Melissa's mom usually only stays for three days, this time she stayed for three weeks. Her mother left only to return for another three week stay.

The people on Melissa's street became a second family to her. "We looked out for each other, made lists of supplies when someone was going out, and brought back what everybody needed," she shared.

Friday after the storm Melissa and her sons began helping Innovative Charities, who gave away food from Second Harvest and other supplies. Although her boys weren't particularly excited about volunteering, she taught them the importance of giving back. "I told them 'we are so blessed that we are fine, the car is fine, the house is fine, we have water and we have everything we need,'" she shared. "We didn't have a generator until the first supplies were delivered to Saint Luke's the following week, I brought a generator to the house," she added.

Melissa worked a little the week of the hurricane with a generator, so that there would be bulletins at church. The second week she was able to work about ten hours. The next week she and her mother worked about twelve hours sorting donations and preparing bulletins. The week after the hurricane she went back to work at the First Presbyterian Church food pantry giving out donations and there was no limit to what was being provided.

"You could come every time we were open and get what you need," she explained.

Photos provided by Melissa Krebeck

Michelle Borden

Michelle Borden and her family stayed the night with her neighbor. It was hot and the windows were open. "One of the most devastating things was that night we could hear someone walking up and down the street calling for their animal," she remembered. "Part of me was like, oh my gosh, stop screaming I'm trying to get my kids to sleep, and the other part of me was like that is horrible!" "I couldn't imagine how it would feel if your animal was lost and you didn't even know if they were alive or dead right now," she recalled. Michelle and her family didn't have any pets, but had been feeding a stray cat. When her children asked her where the cat went, she had to say that she didn't know.

The next morning when they woke up, they couldn't believe their eyes. She recalled thinking "Holy Crap! It's a war zone!" Another neighbor had some large equipment, and Michelle's boyfriend had the hundred pound chains that he had used on the kids' outdoor play-set. The neighbors worked together pulling trees out to form a path. "When we got to the last tree, it was just too big and would have ripped the truck apart!" Meanwhile, her boyfriend went exploring and was able to climb his way through to Lafayette Street that runs through the middle of town. One house he passed was the house Michelle had lived in just three months before that had a wall of glass on one side, only needed the roof to be replaced. He reported back the amount of destruction he had seen. "I thought, I don't know how we are going to get out of here," Michelle explained. She remembers assessing the situation. She needed to get her children out and the neighbor was taking care of an elderly lady, who was incontinent and health was not good. "They tried their hardest to get an ambulance but no one could get through to us," she continued. It took two days before the woman could be rescued.

Meanwhile she was getting calls about not showing up for work. Half of Michelle's coworkers had been at work during the storm and needed to be relieved. One of her coworkers offered to bring a generator, if Michelle would go to her house. She tried to explain that her house was gone, but her friend just offered to let Michelle's family stay with her. What her friend couldn't understand is Michelle couldn't physically leave. They were trapped. Michelle's job was in a recovery effort, which required action within forty-eight hours. Her coworkers were clearing the street to make it happen. Although Michelle was trapped, she felt guilty about her inability to help her coworkers. There was nothing she could do but wait. Their vehicles were okay, except Michelle's had a few scratches but getting out was impossible at that time. "We could hear people with chainsaws, but none of us on our block had a chainsaw," she continued. We had to move limbs out of the driveway to get the cars where they could be driven out, should the road be cleared.

"We were going in and out of the house finishing the puzzle," she recalled. During this time they put food out for the stray cat, which later returned. Michelle's boyfriend's minivan had chargers, which enabled them to charge their cell phones. "My phone was blowing up," she explained. "Finally, we see people coming down West Manor towards Putnam," she continued. Michelle asked the people if they could cut the tree, so she and her neighbors could move it out of the way. The people helped them. It was probably 6 p.m. on Thursday.

They had no idea where they were going to go. All the hotels were full with evacuees and contractors, who had come in to help. Michelle's parents were trying to assist her with obtaining a hotel room within an hour of her job so she could complete her responsibilities and get paid. However, they couldn't find anything either.

Michelle's parents had moved to Crawfordville, which is south of Tallahassee in 2005. While they no longer lived in Crawfordville, they still had a house downtown. Although Crawfordville was nearly two hours away in a different time zone, it seemed to be the only option. So, Thursday night the family left town for Crawfordville. Fortunately, by that time I-10 had been cleared, and they had no trouble getting through. When they traveled within Tallahassee, they didn't see much damage, but everything was dark. There was no electricity. "The only place we could find open to eat was a Zaxbys and it was cash only" she continued. Following the storm all purchases required cash. "I was never one to carry cash, but thankfully, and for some reason, I had gotten cash before the storm." They were able to eat dinner at Zaxbys in Crawfordville. When they arrived at Michelle's parent's home in Crawfordville, Walmart and their home had electricity. The home did not have much in the way of furnishings. "My little brother had just come the month before and taken all the living room furniture," she shared. There were two beds, plenty of linens and a television. So the children took one and the adults slept in the other. They needed food, clothes, toiletries, "I didn't have a hair brush, toothbrush, toothpaste, soap or anything, because it was all under a tree!" Friday morning they discovered there was no food in the house, except food her parents had pickled. The family ate breakfast at Subway and bought about $600 worth of supplies at Walmmart.

During that time, the children's father, who lives in Grand Ridge, Florida had been texting her. He had lost power, but had no major damage to his home. He and the family's dog had survived the storm. His parent's live in Punta Gorda, in south Florida. "He asked me if I wanted him to take the kids and I battled back and forth in my mind," she recalled. While she didn't want to be away from her children, Michelle knew his parents loved and spoiled the kids. She also knew it was in their best interest. So, she met her ex-husband in Tallahassee and he took the children to his parent's house, where they stayed until school started back.

Paula Livergood

After the storm Paula's front door was completely blocked by a fallen Magnolia Tree. "We couldn't even go out, not even three inches," Paula shared. All they could do was open the door. They were able to go out the side door about three or four feet, but then they found out they were blocked on all sides by trees. To make their way to the front yard, Paula and her children had to go out the back door and climb their way over and under fallen trees. "It would wear you out, because some of the trees were probably as much as three feet in diameter," she explained. "There were so many sticks, and you didn't know what else was underneath there," Paula added, "We were stepping over what was left of the fence." The pool chairs and children's toys were scattered on neighboring properties, as well as Paula's roof. Most of the fence was completely gone. "What remained looked as if it had been put through a 'wood chipper,'" she recalled. "Nine months later, I was still finding pieces of the fence," Paula shared. There was a tree on the car and on the garage. There were three trees blocking the driveway. "I had at least fourteen trees down" Paula shared. She could tell where other trees had hit the house and rolled off. Then, as if not enough, Paula's neighbors' trees had fallen in her yard. Her swimming pool, and decks were completely destroyed.

"The day after the hurricane I sat on my porch trying not to let the kids see me upset and crying, because I didn't know what was going to happen," Paula shared. She didn't know the status of her job or how long it would be before she got paid. "I talked to their dad and he offered money to help us tie over," she added. "Then, he started talking about them going out to Arkansas to live with them until school was back in session." Although Paula's children didn't like the idea, she considered it for their well-being. "It scared the devil out of me, because I thought what if they like it better and don't want to come back." She also wondered what would happen if her ex-husband, who is a wonderful father, liked them out there so much, that he would be willing to fight to have them there with him. While she knew he was trying to do the best thing for them, it frightened her. For months she had a strong drive to make their home better to prove to him that it was safe. He was constantly praising her, but the fear remained in the back of her mind. "I almost lost my house and now I'm about to lose my children," she shared. The fear Paula shared came from her intense desire to be a good parent. She was afraid of losing everything important to her.

Danielle and Carlton checking out the damage after the storm. Photos provided by Paula Livergood.

"Thankfully, people like Martin Basford, Mr. Kincaid, Mr. Johnson and other volunteers were cutting people out the day after the storm," she explained. "Then the other folks were coming out asking if we were all safe and seeing what supplies were needed, and checking for survivors." Not being able to access much equipment, the Livergood's began trying to make a path through their yard and on the road, so their neighbors could travel through the path. "I was very proud of my children, because when they started cutting things out, they never complained," she shared. Paula wanted others to know the house wasn't vacant, so she brought out her pool umbrella and other things to ward off looters. "So, I told my son this is like our beacon of hope and sign of life," she continued. "We will be okay and we will rebuild," she added. Paula mounted solar lights on the deck to light up the parcel. Not only did the lights provide an element of safety, but it let others know that the area was cleared for them drive into the neighborhood.

Photo provided by Paula Livergood.

While the Livergood family had most of what they needed, on the third day they were finally able to leave their neighborhood. Paula and children worked two days to make a three foot path from her front door to the street. This path allowed Paula's brother to pick up her children, and her mother, and take them to Dothan. "The only reason we were able to do this is because Martin Basford would come up and cut a little of the big limbs, so we could move them aside," Paula shared.

Her children and mother would stay with Paula's brother for a week. When they returned, it was harder, than if they had stayed after the storm. My daughter went to my mother and started crying saying "I wish Hurricane Michael had never happened," she shared. When Paula's children went to her brother's home it was a load off of her mind because they were safe. However, she wanted them back, but didn't realize how difficult it would be on them when they returned. After they had been away about two weeks her mother also wanted to return. Paula shared that it was so hard for them to learn the new normal, or routine, until power and water was restored. Paula's mother brought out an old German game that helped her daughter, Danielle.

They didn't have land line phone service, Internet or electricity, and Paula was very concerned about her father. While cell phone service would come and go, she received texted photos of her father's house from his neighbors. For at least two days her father had been sending texts saying "I need help," she recalled. The side door and carport to her father's home had fallen and was blocking the entrance. He could only come and go through his front door. When her father was able to leave out the front door, he had to climb over and under fallen trees. Part of a tree had fallen on her father's truck and had completely destroyed his car.

On the third day someone had to cut his truck out. Then, he drove to Paula.

Damaged at her father's home. Photos by Paula Livergood.

Paula needed some supplies from the store. It was extremely hot and the bees, wasps and yellow jackets were bad. Paula had heard about some free food, so her father drove her to Winn Dixie. "It was so surreal to stand in line with all those other people not knowing where we were going to go from here and what might happen," she remembered. Only a few people were allowed in the store at a time, "but to feel that cool air, ahhh," she added, "it was more than getting supplies, it was about resemblance of normalcy and a sign that things will get better."

After picking up supplies, her father had to dodge fallen trees and fallen power lines, and work his way down a path to get to her home. "You couldn't tell that River Forest was even a road anymore," she continued. When they approached the Milton Johnson Health Center, she told her father that she would walk the remainder of the way. While she was walking, she didn't recognize the area because of the devastation. "As I was walking by my home I said 'I wonder whose home that is' and it donged on me that was my house!"

Paula wanted her children to understand about helping others and be thankful what had been provided for them. So for at least a couple of days, the family walked about a half mile to Saint Anne's Catholic Church and worked the food pantry. "I wanted them to see the good that comes out of the hurricane," she added.

Saint Anne's Catholic Church Food Pantry. Photos provided by Paula Livergood.

Some of the church members that lived in an area where they had well water, brought Paula water, gas and other supplies. On the same day one of her neighbor's sons came from Orlando with a truck full of food, water, supplies and generators. They all went down to the neighbor's home where they cooked everything about to spoil in the freezer for a neighborhood feast. "It was a wonderful, wonderful thing," she shared. This would be a story many would share about their neighborhoods.

The Sunday after the Hurricane, Saint Anne's Catholic Church was receiving supplies. Paula was there and hadn't had a shower yet. The only key she had to her home had gotten broken. Her doors were unlocked and the children were in Dothan. She was helping out, and one of the parishioners was going to let her go back with them for a shower. While Paula was there she started getting panicky, because she knew the neighbors and police had discovered a looter walking around in one of the houses on her street heavily damaged by the hurricane. She had also seen many people going through her neighborhood, who had never been there before. "Some of them looked unsavory with their cameras out recording and taking photos of our neighborhood," she continued. "I went from so excited to being out from my house for a while, to scared to death to be away from home," she shared.

Just before she was about to walk home, someone at church helped Paula load up supplies and drove her home. "For a while it was hard for me to be away from the house because of the fear of going through that," she explained. "I felt so vulnerable and open to what could happen." "I had survived the hurricane, but there were still dangers out there that lurked," Paula added.

"It was hard returning to work the following week, because I knew there was so much that needed to be done at my dad's house and mine," she shared. His home wasn't safe. A tree had fallen in her father's house and the ceiling had collapsed in his bedroom. He was sleeping on the floor. Water kept coming into his house. He had huge trash cans and buckets collecting the water and he would need help dumping it out because it was so heavy.

At the same time Paula looked forward to returning to work, because it was a little normalcy in her life and she wanted to try to help other people through work. She had the generator and it was a little cooler, but her kids had already left for Dothan. Paula created a new routine of returning home after work. She would make sure the generator was running, and turn on some lights. Then, she would walk the dogs and make sure they were fed. Paula was able to fill up jugs of water for her dogs at her father's house, because he had City of Marianna water.

She didn't have water for over eight days. On the tenth day one of the neighbors hooked up the generator to their community well so that every couple of days for an hour they could have water. "We would quickly refill our jugs and bathtubs, and flush the toilet," she shared. "At night I would be so hot and filthy that

I would lay in the cold, cold bathtub." Paula, like many others, created a system for what was her new normal. Then, she would fall asleep at 7 pm on the living room sofa because she had a fan. With her generator she was able to run one fan, one lamp, the refrigerator and a charging station for her cell phone.

"My supervisor was wonderful picking me up and taking me to work," she shared. Her father's truck was not running well the week after the storm, and his car was completely destroyed. "By the time they pulled his car out, it was no more than twenty-four inches high," she shared. "We couldn't even see where the steering wheel was." "They asked us to leave the keys in the car," she continued, "and I said okay, but I don't know where the ignition is!" Paula remembered how Hurricane Michael had pulled off one of the car doors and thrown it into the bushes.

"I was so worried because he didn't have a car and I didn't have a car," she continued "and people kept saying 'you need to go get these supplies.'" While people did help her pick up supplies, she'd only have so much room, because they were picking up their supplies too. "Knowing I needed to get my own transportation, I asked my ex-husband to help look for me a car," Paula shared. "I had gone online and found one I liked in Dothan," she continued. "My supervisor was so nice." she shared. "She let me off early and drove me to my dad's house." Paula had her purse and backpack that had all her insurance and paperwork in it. "My backpack and my purse was like my lifeline that whole week when people would give me rides," she continued.

Paula's vehicle after Hurricane Michael. Photo provided by Paula Livergood.

Paula's dad was going to drive her to Dothan, but his truck was acting up. Her best friend was going to pick her up at his house, but they were running late for a doctor's appointment. Paula's father was able to drive her to Greenwood to her friend's house. Then, Paula rode with her friend to the doctor's office and called the dealership from there. "I said 'can somebody come pick me up?'" "They said 'what if you don't buy this car?'" Paula continued. She told them that she would find a way back home.

The salesperson picked her and took her to get something to eat. "This was the fourth person helping me to get to the dealership," she shared. "It took four people to get me to the dealership and they were so nice." "I was just so happy to be in the air conditioning," she added. They told Paula she could watch television, but she said, "I'm used to no t.v. by now, and I don't need it." A few hours later, she was driving off the lot with her new car.

Paula went to her brother's house and to see her kids and mother. "I said 'why don't we go have a nice dinner to celebrate?'" Paula and her family went to a Chinese restaurant. "We were sitting there and I kept wondering why the ticket wasn't coming, so I asked for it," Paula continued. The server explained that her ticket had already been paid. When she finally figured out which family had paid, she went to them. "He said 'your children were so polite and helping others so much that I thought, I want to pay for them,'" she remembered. Paula explained to the man how much the gesture meant since they had no electricity, water, cable or Internet at home, and her children were staying in Dothan where it was safe, while she was working at home. "Along the way everyone had been so nice and so supportive" she shared. "People came from out of town to help us and feed us, which was one less meal that I had to worry about," she explained. "It was really touching, because it was so stressful and still is."

Shelby Durham

By Friday Shelby and her family had seen photos on television and social media showing the storm damage. Shelby was unable to contact any of her neighbors, and was anxious to see if their home was still there. Matthew's parents requested a neighbor walk to their newly reroofed home to see if it had survived the brutal storm. They were happy to find out their home was untouched. All the trees had fallen south away from their home.

It was nearly a week before Matthew and Shelby could travel into Bay County to see the status of their home. However, she remembered a website being released with aerial photography of the area. "I could tell the house was standing and trees were down, but I could see a big hole in the roof." "When we got down there we realized the house was unlivable." The storm had blown the barn down and the shed was gone. Inside the house Shelby noticed mold already starting to develop on the vents and water spots all over the ceiling. The hallway doors had swelled from being wet and would no longer shut. The storm had lifted the tile off the floor. The couple was told that the two holes in the roof prevented the entire roof from coming off.

"You never leave your house thinking that this is going to be your last time," Shelby explained. "I can remember it just like it was yesterday, pulling out of the driveway, and thinking my husband was crazy for making us evacuate," she shared. "Not having a clue that the night before was my last night sitting in my living room, eating ice cream, watching Netflix and the last time we were in that house," she continued. "It's just surreal."

Photos of devastation in the neighborhood where Matthew's parents live.
Photos provided by Shelby Durham.

Matthew and Shelby did not know what they were going to do. In addition, Shelby was in the early stages of pregnancy and didn't know yet. While having no plans to return to Marianna, they knew that they needed to stay with Matthew's parents at least for a while. She was unable to keep her job in Panama City, which she loved.

She recalled returning to Marianna, where they had lived ten years prior. The couple had enjoyed living in Panama City, because there were many things to do as a young couple. Yet, they knew they didn't want to a raise a family there. "I knew our time there was temporary, but didn't know how soon that was going to come to pass," she shared.

When they pulled back into Marianna, they couldn't drive in. They had to walk. The street was covered with debris and fallen trees. Shelby and Matthew helped his family move trees and limbs in the extreme heat following Hurricane Michael. After they had cleared the road to a path, so that people could come in and out, a man from south Florida came in with equipment and quoted them six hundred dollars to remove a tree the family was unable to remove. "It made me mad because he was taking advantage of our situation," she continued.

Photos of the devastation in Matthew's parent's neighborhood in Marianna.
Photos provided by Shelby. Durham.

"Then, we had these gentlemen walk up, who had been in the Carolinas working endlessly after another hurricane and heard about Michael," she continued. The men had decided they would travel down to Marianna and help. "They were sleeping in their truck and heating their food on the motor," she shared. "They cut that tree for us for free." "They were here with the intention of cutting people out of their homes, who needed help for nothing in return," she added. Mathew, the men and a few others went south of town and continued helping people, who were trapped. "They weren't here to get rich off of our despair," she remembered.

Shelby's father came down and helped the couple move what was left in their home. Finding a storage building was impossible at that time and storage building space was nearly impossible to find. "When we moved down to Marianna, we moved in with Matthew's parents and everything went into Packrat," she explained. "Then, after Hurricane Michael, we moved back in with Matthew's parents, and all our belongings went back to Packrat," she continued. "We'd made a full circle."

During that time she remembered "like clockwork at curfew generators would come on, and 6 a.m. you would hear chainsaws all day." "The first time we heard Waffle House was open we went in, and the people were so friendly and uplifting," she recalled. "I cried because I had not seen electricity in days and had been eating beanie weenies," Shelby shared. "It was a taste of normalcy that I had taken for granted." "Nobody ever thinks that this will happen to them."

Ronnie Keel

Ronnie was trapped in his house for two days. Dianna, his wife, called from Tennessee and told him how many holes were in the roof. "Somebody, evidently, had a drone and was flying over things," he shared laughing. He had supplies, and cell phone service. The second day someone brought him a generator to use.

James had to move Catherine out of the home, because she couldn't be cared for within the house that was falling down around them. In the eye of the storm, Ronnie had called his oldest daughter, who tried to get Catherine some help, but first responders couldn't reach her because the roads were all blocked. "The second night some of his grandkids had come, and took a chainsaw and cut a path to South Street," Ronnie continued. "The firemen come around in the middle of the night and carried Catherine 200 yards or more to South Street to load her in an ambulance going to Chipley," he added. The hospital in Chipley was the closest one that would take her. "I didn't see him anymore for about three weeks because he was with her," Ronnie explained. "I talked to him on the phone and told him I would watch out for everything."

Ronnie shared that as soon as the roads were opened up enough on Friday, he traveled to his farm south of town. From there he was able to retrieve his fish cooker and bring it back for cooking. "It was amazing to me the speed in which they opened roads back up." "As soon as the storm was out, I dare say there was anywhere in the County where you could go more than a mile down any road," Ronnie added. "By Friday you had to drive around things, but they had it where you could go in and out." Ronnie had hot water the entire time and a cellular signal most of the time. While he was able to watch television with his generator, he could only watch recordings. "I really missed not seeing what the news footage was," he shared. "You always watch what is happening to someone else, somewhere else, but when it's on you, you can't tell," he continued. "The ones that need to know don't know." About three weeks after the storm power was returned to Ronnie and Dianna's home in Marianna. Ronnie went on to share that he had never seen anything like this storm, and never wanted to see it again.

Ronnie's wife Dianna, and youngest daughter, Amanda, returned with the grandchildren about five days after the storm. Ronnie shared that the aftermath of Hurricane Michael was more upsetting to Dianna, than the storm itself had been for him. Amanda lives near Ronnie and Dianna's farm. Ronnie described that while Amanda was away, her home had survived with roof damage. Also, Amanda's shed was destroyed. She had plenty of trees down, but was blessed that none had hit her home. Prior to the storm, Ronnie had staked down the trampoline Amanda's children played on. "I don't think they know yet where it's at," he shared.

The farm animals and fencing survived fine. A portion of the roof was blown off his barn, and an enclosed portion collapsed. "All and all, the damage to the barn was very little compared to what I expected it to be," he explained. Ronnie went on to explain that a tree had fallen across his equipment shed and destroyed it. Hurricane Michael took out two thirds of the pines on Ronnie's farm, which he was right before thinning. A year later Ronnie explained that he still hasn't seen the biggest portion of the farm because there are trees across the internal roads.

About three days after the storm, Ronnie's friend Graham Dozier, who lives in Wewahitchka, came toward Marianna looking for fuel for a generator. Graham traveled close enough to call Ronnie. "He had some damage at his home, but not catastrophic," Ronnie shared. "He had just loss of trees, siding torn from the house and roof torn up and such," he explained. Ronnie shared that Graham had electricity in Wewahitchka before he did in Marianna.

Photos provided by Amanda Keel McCoy.

Ronnie and Dianna's son, Ron and his wife, Cheryl live near
the Florida State University Panama City Campus. They decided
to ride out Hurricane Michael at their home. After the storm
Dianna and Amanda began trying to contact Ron and Cheryl.
Communication after Hurricane Michael was poor, and Dianna
was unable to determine whether or not the couple was safe.

"The   thing   that   was   catastrophically   bad   was
communications," Ronnie shared. "The police, first responders
and people couldn't communicate with one another because
everything was blown out." "After the first day, Dianna could
call me from Tennessee, but I couldn't call Graham or Jimmy . . .

[another friend] . . . or Ron," he continued. "Sustained winds were a category five, but the gusts were way beyond that." "The big pine tree in the back yard, it blew the top out of it 40 yards into James' house," he added.

It was about a week later before Ronnie and Dianna would know that their son and daughter-in-law were safe. Amanda's friend, who lived in Tennessee, owned property on Panama City Beach. He was in communication with some people in Panama City. Whenever he was able to drive in, he searched for Ron and Cheryl. "I hadn't talked to them since about an hour before the hurricane made landfall," Ronnie remembered. "Ron and Cheryl had been driving around the beach looking at the waves," he continued. "I told him you better get across the bridge before they shut the bridge down." The Hathaway Bridge would be shut down once winds reached a certain speed. Ron had explained that it was getting gusty and he was headed towards his home. About a week later Ronnie and Dianna learned that Ron and Cheryl had been trapped in their home and were finally getting out.

"I didn't see any looters and the amount of volunteer help was just unbelievable" Ronnie shared. "For more than a month there was more people wanting to do things to help you than you could shake a stick at!" "There's bad people in the world, but there's a whole lot of good people too," he continued. "There's a whole lot more good people that there is bad people!" "My oldest daughter even came by with food and water on her go-cart," he said laughing. "Probably the most inconvenient thing of all was ice."

James Lash

A tree company came through and cut the trees off James' property while he was at the Chipley Hospital with his wife. The company was unable to collect from James' insurance company. James had to hire an attorney because the company was threatening to sue him for $27 thousand." "They are saying that I was in breach of contract, but I didn't know the people were there until three days after it was over with," James shared. "The only people I called was the insurance company!" "There was no phone service in Chipley," he continued explaining they would have had to contact him through the hospital.

"Ronnie . . . [Keel] . . . was just blessed," he shared. "The one tree that didn't fall was a huge, huge tree that had died," he continued. "It stood there."

James shared that every tree Ronnie and Debbie Lollie had was down, but their house was fine. Like everyone else, they didn't have electrical power. James stayed with Catherine at the Chipley hospital for two weeks before staying in a Tallahassee motel for two weeks.

Ronstance Pittman

The next day Ronstance and her husband found a man selling generators on the side of the road and bought one. They removed water from their swimming pool to flush the toilet. "It was a little awkward because we were newlyweds only living in the house together for a couple of months." Ronstance explained how toting the water upstairs reminded her of what it must have been like for her forefathers who had to carry water because they had no running water. "We did that for two weeks," she explained. Ronstance shared that they had water and electricity after two weeks.

Gas was scarce. Ronstance had an older black car. Before the storm they had fueled up her main car and his car, which couldn't move. So, they needed to fill up the black car. The couple had heard there was gas in Campbellton. Despite her warning her new husband that they wouldn't make it that far, they headed towards Campbellton. The car ran out of gas just as they were approaching the overpass. She sat in the car and her new husband walked to the gas station. While he was gone, her cousins came by and she went with them to Dothan for gas. Her husband was left waiting outside a locked car until she returned an hour or more later. She didn't even leave a note. Once she had cellular service, she notified him.

Ronstance's mom lives in Jacob and she had electricity after a week, and had water the entire time. A couple of cousins that live in Atlanta cut a path down her mother's dirt road to her home. Then, she went home on a tractor, because she had water. So the family would go over and take cold showers, and later warm showers at her mom's house.

They also went back and forth to her mother's church. Ronstance orchestrated a hot meal location at the church and they cooked for the community. They also had shipments of supplies from FAMU, Convoy of Hope, and the Sorority Alpha Kappa Alpha. They basically setup a distribution at her mother's church. They serviced a large area. Shaleigh shared how churches were doing what God planned for them to do, provide a helping hand to those in need

Carmen Smith

Thursday morning Carmen and her fiancé traveled about 60 miles, which took four and a half hours that day to arrive at Indian Springs just east of Marianna. When she arrived in Jackson County, she recalled "without knowing where I was, I wouldn't have recognized anything." "Seeing all the homes destroyed and the gas stations toppled over, it was something unreal at that time." "I think I started crying when I saw Grand Ridge until I got home," she shared. She recalled almost missing the turn into her subdivision, because it looked completely different.

When Carmen saw the damage on her home, she remembered crying more. She had lots of fallen trees. One hit the front of her home and took up her septic tank. Another tree had fallen on the back. She was in shock. "I was literally fighting the tree debris to even get to my back door," she explained. All other doors to the home were inaccessible. For the first couple of weeks, this was how Carmen and her fiancé entered the house. They returned to Tallahassee that night to contact the insurance company and get everything in order.

While everyone was experiencing emotional trauma of some type, they were evaluating their particular circumstances and looking for ways to improve their situations. They found hope in God and helping one another in the earliest moments. Then, they would find hope in the first responders

Chapter Six

First Things First

While residents were assessing their situations, first responders were eager to start working. The biggest problem faced was clearing the roads so citizens could be helped. Also on the list of priorities keeping water, sewer and natural gas utilities functioning. Clear roads and operational utilities were essential, especially to the local hospital and nursing homes. With the heat pounding down after the storm return of electricity was important too. However, clearing the roads, maintaining and restoring utilities and providing cellular services required fuel, which was in high demand. Also in high demand was ice. Despite never living through a disaster of this magnitude or having experience in making the necessary decisions. First responders and officials came together and made the best possible decisions.

Mayor Roberts

Mayor Roberts stayed at home with his wife and oldest son Russell during the storm. He shared that the first thing he noticed was the big transmission lines near his home all fell down.

Then, they watched as all the trees fell on top of the transmission lines. He explained that they still had cell phone service in the eye when his neighbor, Jerry Glass, called saying there was nothing to worry about. "I said, 'Jerry we're in the eye!'" he recalled laughing. Mayor Roberts went on to share that Jerry took his advice and stayed inside. "When the storm was over, we had a lot of trees down, but our house was not damaged," he continued. The family decided to walk to Russell's house, which is about 300 yards east of their home. The Mayor shared how it took about an hour walking and climbing over and under trees. "It was just one more mess trying to get that short little distance." When they arrived, at first they thought there was no damage to Russell's house because the front looked pristine. "But when we walked to the back of his house, Russell had three large pine trees that bordered his house and all three had fallen in the back of his house!" Since that time Russell has been living with them in the upstairs of their house, but is supposed to move back home soon.

Photos of the demolished Madison's Warehouse Restaurant.
Photos provided by Rhonda Dykes.

"Basically, I started by calling Jim Dean," Mayor Roberts shared. "Everything was just in chaos, but we went out to the emergency center the county had set up, and talked with them there," he continued. Among the first people Mayor Roberts talked to after the storm were his neighbors Ricky Miller and Robert Reiff. "There was a big caterpillar tractor where they were doing work at Chipola on those retention ponds and a trooper got in the caterpillar and cleared up to Jefferson Street with it." This allowed the emergency responders at Chipola College to access Cavern's Road.

"When we came down that morning after the storm, you could see Madison's was totally demolished" he explained. Madison's Warehouse Restaurant shared a common wall with the Roberts, Roberts and Roberts' office. "When we opened our building, we didn't even have a leak, no roof damage, no water damage, nothing!" Mayor Roberts continued, "of course, now, my sons owned that big building on Lafayette Street that was blown down and some of the bricks were found in the second story of the Court House", which is across the four-laned Lafayette street that runs through the middle of Marianna. "We had to hire a specialty company out of Tallahassee, named Southern Demolition, to tear the building down," he continued. They didn't have insurance on the building and it cost them $72,500 to remove the dilapidated structure and haul off the debris.

The City Manager had shared with the Mayor that there were generators at our wells, but the pressure wasn't what it should be. Yet, staff was able to find the leak somewhere around Chipola College and repair it. The water pressure returned. On Friday, Betty Demmon and others at WJAQ were set up in the Century Link building. "Russell was with me and Betty put me on the air to let everyone know what was going on," the Mayor shared. "Then Russell put it out on Facebook," he explained. This was a great way to maximize media coverage and to reach as many people as possible.

"We finally got a generator hooked up to our house after two or three days," Mayor Roberts explained. On Sunday Mayor Roberts stood up in the First Methodist Church, where he is a member, and gave a report about what the City was doing and the recovery effort time frame.

"Everybody was really great, including the people that brought us the generator that allowed us to continue to operate out of City Hall," he shared. During those first days there were numerous meetings with staff and about debris pickup. The Mayor shared how debris haulers wanted the City to hire them, but through the County, the Florida Department of Transportation started the debris cleanup. "And we are still cleaning up," he continued.

"I was just very impressed with how Jim and all the department heads handled everything," he shared. "It was unbelievable." The Mayor shared how there wasn't even any fuel here. People traveled to Dothan, Alabama to purchase fuel for the vehicles and their generators with cash.

"I've had relatives who have lived in Jackson County since 1821 and nobody has ever experienced anything like this" the Mayor shared. Mayor Robert's grandmother, a Kent, arrived in Jackson County in 1821. He went on to explain that "I'm 76 years old and we've gone through some hurricanes, but we've never had anything like this!" He shared, "nobody expected this."

"It was amazing how quiet it got when the eye came over and to watch those huge Gulf Power transmission lines fall," he added. "They fell before the trees fell."

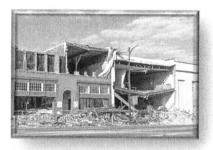

Above: Photos of the building owned by the Mayor's sons that had to be demolished. **Below**: The Jackson County Court House Square, where bricks were found upstairs. Photos provided by Rhonda Dykes.

Commissioner Williams

Commissioner Williams and his family were unable to get home for a day. Checking on his home the day after entailed walking and climbing over and under trees, and then catching a ride. He was unable to drive out from Bellamy Bridge Road because of all the trees down. When he arrived at Clay Street, where he lives, he remembered "all the neighbors got together and cleared our road." He felt blessed that there were trees down all over the place, but none on his house. "A portion of his foundation came up," he shared, "but not any topical structure damage."

After he made it home, Commissioner Williams organized a group of kids who would clean a path to their church. They also cleaned up a few elderly ladies' yards, so they could get out of their driveways. "Once we got the road done, we just tried to help out the elderly in the neighborhood."

Not surprisingly Commissioner Williams' children Imani (17) and Corey (13) wanted to help after the storm. They wanted to pass out food and do whatever they could to help others. "And they were keeping me straight," he added.

His wife, Rebekah, who is a nurse for the VA, was busy passing out food and helping in the church. "I asked her 'you didn't eat?'" He continued. "She said 'no because there were so many people who needed it more, that I didn't want to think about myself.'" He remembered his family going to find something to eat after feeding thousands of people. When she returned to work, they had make-shift tents up, so they could care for the veterans. "They really did a good job making the vets feel comfortable," he shared.

"Starting the second day after the storm, we met every day at City Hall," he shared. He remembered how Police Chief Baggett recommended a curfew from 6 p.m. to 6 a.m., which curbed a lot of crime that could have happened. "I think that was one of the most important decisions that we made." He also shared how the Fire Chief played an important role in distributing blue tarps, which are still visible today. He recalled how everyone was working together.

"One thing I was proud of was our City workers who worked tirelessly hour after hour not even knowing if they would be paid." "I really can't think of one that refused," he added.

During the time without electricity, Commissioner Williams purchased generators. However, he explained that when the fuel ran out or you had to leave the house, there was a fear that someone would steal your generator. He remembered, as the man of the house, not getting any sound sleep or rest for over a month.

Jim Dean, City Manager

When the storm was over, City Manager Jim Dean noticed a bunch of trees were down, one of which was very large. He saw ditch water in his swimming pool and his fence was damaged. However, his biggest concern was that the City would be without water and sewer. With a backpack strapped on, Jim climbed over trees, across power lines and hiked across the City to the Wastewater Treatment Plant. Along the way, he cut trees out of the way. "We never lost water, waste water and natural gas in the City of Marianna," Jim shared proudly. After resting at the Wastewater Treatment Plant, Jim returned to City Hall and began trying to figure out what to do next. One of the most important items on his list was cleaning roads. Within a few days City Hall was opened for a point of information. "The City of Marianna Police, Fire and Public Works Departments never stopped!" Only five days after the storm, critical personnel returned to work. "We had daily meetings, which later became weekly communications, to help relieve stress," Jim explained. Yard trash collection was deferred for three to four months, garbage collection for two months and billing for utilities was deferred for two months.

Jim shared how he would have never imagined so much damage. Still it never crossed his mind to leave behind his beloved City. "If we had not had so many trees, we would not have seen so much damage," Jim stated. "All the damaged houses and downtown makes me nauseous!"

Marianna Public Works Department

After the storm, Joe made his way to well five to meet with Rick and ensure everything was running. "There were trees down on every road," Joe explained. "Well five had damage but no interference with treatment," Rick continued, "but the telemetry was not working." Rick and Doug had their employees out with chainsaws and backhoes at 4 a.m. trying to get the roads cleared of debris. "It took almost seven hours to clear from the old Marianna High School to River Road," (approximately ten blocks) Doug explained. "We were trying to keep water to the area around the hospital and Marianna Health and Rehab to keep the well running," shared Rick. The guys did a good job because Marianna Health and Rehab did not have to be evacuated. Doug shared how his guys made sure natural gas was operational because the City's well generators were fueled by natural gas. Doug continued, "we had 35 total natural gas service lines damaged." "To make matters worse, there were people on social media spreading untrue rumors, although we were already going above industry standards on depth," Doug added. The natural gas fueling station was another priority, because Waste Pro fueled there and they needed to be available to remove debris.

Jim Dean shared one of his most hair-raising memories was when the power company contracted under Florida Public Utilities was trying to install a pole in the ground near the intersection of Orange Street and Old Cottondale Road at the railroad tracks. Their auger made punctures into a four inch gas line with 125 pounds of pressure. Leon County helped with the three block neighborhood evacuation. Jim watched as Doug Glass, Natural Gas Supervisor and Lee Hunter were working on the line. "Suddenly there was a loud swooshing sound as natural gas escaped so fast as to make Doug and Lee's hair stand straight up!" "They worked on it all night and Doug brought in Rave Construction, an expert gas contractor, who helped remedy the situation," Jim recalled. "We had help from TECO Gas on locating utilities after the Orange Street incident," Doug added.

The Public Works Department was blessed to have Destin Water Users, Mossy Head and South Walton Utilities come in and help gain access to utilities. Thirty-five lift stations needed access to hook up portable generators at each lift station. Pinellas County brought in generators and generator technicians. They also assisted in providing a City escort 24 hours a day, and split their days. They had meetings daily at shift change. "The Pinellas County generator technicians took a lot of pressure off the City Manager, Public Works Director and myself," Rick shared. "They were great!" "They never complained, slept in tents and showered at the Waste Water Treatment Plant," Rick added.

Destin brought in chainsaws to help get to the well sites and to fuel the generators. Water was the first priority. So, Public Works employees developed a 24 hour a day fueling cycle, including Sunland Training Center. Recreation and Administrative staff assisted. "We saw the Governor four or five times," Rick added. Joe scheduled the Wastewater treatment plant and larger wells with FEMA fixed generators. They worked twelve on and twelve off for two weeks.

The Marianna Municipal Airport also had to be fully functional, which was made possible by a natural gas generator which ran for 27 days. The City's airport became the logistical support area for pod distribution. People were flying in supplies to Marianna and delivering supplies to other areas, including pet food, personal hygiene supplies, food, water and similar needs. Foresters from Oregon coordinated disaster relief for the community. Joe coordinated fuel delivery from FEMA, who understood the importance of diesel fuel. They brought in tankers and gas. Doug shared, "Governor Rick Scott provided a generator for the City's fuel farm in just a matter of hours." "Governor Scott was concerned about Sunland Training Center," Joe added. "This in turn helped get power to the airport," explained Doug. The airport was very important throughout the initial responses.

Another concern was repairing all power lines to the lift stations. Rick and his staff had to stay ahead of the power company to make repairs on weather heads. This would allow for an immediate hook up when the line men arrived. "We coordinated hourly with Florida Public Utilities," Rick explained.

Coordination was key to every step of the disaster response. "Joe was a vital aspect to the entire operation," Doug shared. Rick commented how "Jim was walking across town with a backpack to check on us".

Sam remembered how they were still trying to get to the large equipment at Chipola. He explained, "by the time we got around there, we saw where the storm had took one of those portable buildings and it had disintegrated in the middle of the road." When they finally were able to reach the backhoe, they could see and hear the State Troopers on the other side of the college. "I told them 'I take my hat off to you because I've never known State Troopers to use chainsaws!'" "They were out there elbow-to-elbow with us clearing roads," he continued. "I even went to one of their lieutenants later on and told him how I applaud the Florida State Troopers, because they went above and beyond what I thought a Florida State Trooper would do." "We were finally able to cut some of that stuff loose, when another crew came up and they had a little bobcat," Sam continued. "The bobcat wasn't moving it, but with the backhoe we were able to start moving debris out of the way," he expressed.

Meanwhile, Sam and the other men continued clearing Jefferson Street making their way up to City Hall. "So, we cut

132

through that gauntlet of trees, but the biggest concern was the power grid, because we didn't know which lines were hot," he shared. "We made it through the power grid by the grace of God!" At City Hall the Fire Department joined in and they checked power lines with a fire stick that would identify the ones that were still energized. The men turned onto Lafayette Street and there was debris everywhere. "Our emphasis then was to get the road open to Jackson Hospital, so if anybody was hurt, Fire and Rescue would be able to get them to the hospital," Sam recalled. "We turned onto Guyton Street and the Fire Department checked one of the lines, and it was still a little hot." The Marianna Fire Department called Florida Public Utilities, who gave a timeframe for shutting down the entire grid. "Thank God for that!"

"At that point we were trying to cut the trees where we could take the loader and open up the road so a vehicle could get through," Sam continued. "We weren't trying to clear the roads, but cut openings in the road." At the corner of 2nd Avenue and 6th Street there was a big pine tree laying across the top of the house. "A guy came out from around the back and said he thought there was a family in there," Sam shared. The Fire Department and Charlie went to check on the family, but they found no one at the house. "I said thank God, because the house was crushed."

"When we finally made it through, and it was about 3 a.m." Sam explained. "Part of the hospital roof was gone." By this time Sam and Charlie were exhausted. So, they returned to the shelter where their families were located to make sure they were okay and sleep for a couple hours.

"At 5 o'clock, I said 'Charlie are you ready to go?'" Their goal was to get to the Public Works building on South Street, where they could pick up some equipment. The two men began working their way down Jefferson Street to South Street with the front-end loader. "It was a battle," Sam explained. "Once we were able to get to South Street, we were able to get with different guys and they started trickling in," he elaborated. "Charlie and I the first couple of days worked about twenty hours." Despite the danger, they kept moving forward. "We had to do what we had to do," Sam shared. "We knew our family was fine, so we just stayed at the Public Works Building and took cat naps." Not only did the Public Works Building have a generator, but there was water and restroom facilities. It would be two or three months before Sam would take a day off.

It took Sam two days to cut his way to his own home, so his family could return to their house. Once he had his family home, he purchased a big generator so that his family would have electric power. The generators that some people, like Sam, were able to obtain, would run the basics, such as a refrigerator and lights in a couple of rooms, not full electricity in the house. His down time was spent trying to find gas for the generator and make sure his family had food. "We were in survival mode." Soon a path was opened up to Dothan, Alabama and his wife went back and forth picking up supplies, as needed. "We were without power for over two weeks." Sam's neighbor and "best buddy", Willie Earl Paramore, had natural gas. "Every evening he would tell us 'I got the showers ready" and there would be towels, soap and everything we needed," Sam shared. "He's just a great guy!" "This was a time when neighbors really had to be neighbors" he continued.

Sam explained that after living through Hurricane Andrew, he understood storm survival. "That was a blessing that God had allowed me to go through that before." "Andrew got more structure damage," Sam explained. "Here, I believe what saved the structures was the trees," he continued. "The trees were a blessing and a burden." "When we came down by Sheffield lift station on Old US Road, it was like God laid the trees down in the front of them, in the side of them, and in the back of them" he continued. "But God didn't let them trees fall on the houses." The trees broke the wind, but everyone was trapped. "I believe that if we hadn't had as many trees as we did, Marianna would have been destroyed." "There was a guy that worked for Waste Pro that lived on twenty acres" Sam shared. "It took him two weeks to cut his way out of his yard." The man only had a small chainsaw and the property was covered with fallen trees.

Marianna Fire Department

According to Clint, right after the storm on Wednesday night the Fire personnel went out. "Captain DeLoach called and said 'listen, we can't get out to do anything,'" Clint shared. Trees were down everywhere and they were anxious to start working. "We tried to hold them at bay for a little while, just because we needed to assess the situation," he continued. They had a hot stick, so they could identify hot lines.

"One of the guys from Road and Bridge and one of the guys from Florida Public Utilities knew how to operate some of the heavy equipment in the County yard," Clint explained. "They used a combination of heavy equipment and chainsaws to cut a path down Panhandle Road," he continued. "We finally got out of there about midnight."

Photo provided by Clint Watson.

Clint and others came back on Lafayette Street looking at all the damage. "I've never ever seen anything like this," Clint shared. "When I saw downtown, I thought it would never ever be the same," he laughed emotionally. "It's totally different!" "When he arrived downtown, there was a car in the middle of the street," he shared. "Someone was driving it, got out around Russ Street and took off." As it turned out, the driver was nineteen year old Joshua Glass, son of Gas Divison Supervisor, Doug Glass. Joshua, a CNA at a local nursing home, had been called to work due the emergency during the middle of Hurricane Michael coming through town.

"We were driving and trying to make our way towards the hospital when Wayne Chambliss's brother, who works for Anderson Columbia stopped us in the middle of the street," Clint shared. He explained that if they could get him back to Anderson Columbia, he would help with some heavy equipment to start clearing the roads. Clint's supervisor talked to the head person from Anderson Columbia, who gave him permission to use the piece of equipment. They drove the guy out there to pick up the equipment. Then they started clearing Lafayette Street to make a path to the hospital. Some of the crew that was on duty was already over at the hospital cutting their way in.

Captain Brice Phillips and his wife sheltered at the Public Safety Building at Chipola College with other first responder families. The public safety building held up well, but Brice shared the doors were flying open. When the storm was over they were all anxious to begin helping the community but there was no way out. "We saw lights and walked from the college to Tom Thumb," Brice explained. Brice and the others climbed through fallen trees trying to help open the way. "There was one chainsaw and forty troopers," Brice continued, "and we were like, 'we are coming to get y'all.'" Brice explained the first night he cleared and dug the way to Jackson Hospital with Gulf Coast Utility Company's equipment that had been parked at Chipola College due to work taking place on a Stormwater facility.

The morning after the storm he left Chipola College to find one of the Chambliss boys and to find out how his house had faired during the storm. His supervisor requested he ride out to Anderson Columbia and get a piece of equipment to help clear the streets of Marianna. He followed the instructions provided and met a man who worked for Anderson Columbia. The gentleman told Brice that he could have anything he wanted as long as Brice went to get the keys out of the man's camper on the plant, if it was still there after the storm. The very nice man told Brice that all the keys for everything were in his camper at Anderson Columbia. "He said if the camper is still there you can have all the keys you want," Brice shared. Together they waded through the swamp and climbed over fallen trees to find the camper. "When we got there the trees had perfectly laid down around and away from the camper." "Not a single scratch was on that camper," he continued. The man went in and got the keys. Then, they had to work their way back out of the woods and swamp.

By the time Brice got back, his supervisor was waiting at Anderson Columbia for him. They walked over to a large piece of equipment. "I climbed up in that joker and it had joystick controls in it," Brice explained. "I said 'oh boy I ain't never gotten hold of one with joy stick controls before, but I guess this will be a learning experience!'" "So I got up in there and tried to figure out how to operate it," he explained. The man at Anderson Columbia gave Brice a crash course and told him that was the best he knew how to do. Brice said "alright, I'll figure the rest of it out I guess, and off we went." He made his way back to town and fueled the equipment up at Jackson County Road and Bridge. "After that Billy Baxley kept coming with the City truck, and fueling me up," Brice continued.

There were two pieces of equipment. One fire department crew was trying to cut their way into the hospital and Brice was driving the other piece of equipment. They worked until about 3 a.m. When they finally had a path cut into the hospital, the firemen learned that the top floor of the hospital was leaking and they were not accepting any more patients because of the power situation. At that point any injuries had to be taken somewhere else. It would be a couple of days before the ambulances could run because of the roadway situation. Fire trucks were also limited in where they could travel. "At that point the first priority was to open the roads so you could get to people," Clint explained. Search and rescue was not feasible at that time. So they rested at the station until about 5 a.m. and went back to clear some more.

As soon as they possibly could, fire personnel checked on the conditions of Station Two. Since it had faired-well, and there was plenty of parking, it became a staging area for Florida Public Utilities. Thursday evening, a group of ten engines came from South Florida with thirty personnel and they slept on cots in the fire bay. These firefighters have been training to help in these types of situations. They came in and immediately put together a search and rescue plan, working with the City of Marianna firefighters. The teams were comprised of Marianna firefighters, who knew the area, and the support firefighters, who were trained in search and rescue. They marked each zone off as they went through the areas. Clint explained that a great deal of his time was spent on coordination of the teams. As the crews returned, they would report needs the citizens had, such as water, oxygen and similar items. Then, Clint went to work coordinating follow ups on the requests. "I made a lot of good friends during that time," Clint shared. Some engines were staged at Chipola College, others at City Hall and some at the Jackson County's staging area.

138

"Honestly, as many trees were down, we really thought we were going to be finding a lot of dead people," he continued. "We did run a lot of medical calls, as they were doing search and rescue, that would find people hurt and injured," Clint added. By that time the roads were getting opened back up so they could respond to the medical needs. "I remember going over to South Street, where we had to go through woods walking over and crawling under trees to get to a patient and tote her out to an ambulance," he added.

"The majority of the injuries resulting in deaths were not from the storm itself, but from the cleanup," he explained. People were cutting trees and the trees would fall on them. "The way the trees were twisted, when you cut one, it didn't do what you expected." "There was so much tension on them that they would come back and snap, break and kick back," he continued. Most people had not seen trees twisted and gnarled like this before and did not realize the dangers associated with removing the trees themselves.

All of the Marianna Fire Department worked very hard and tirelessly daily. Clint's son, Brandon, had stayed at a Church in town, and Clint had checked on him via text during the storm and immediately following the storm in person. Brandon was worried about his sister who had stayed at his mobile home. Brandon remained in town, and helped the Marianna Fire Department until later in the afternoon on the day following the storm. Then, he went to check on his sister. His sister and the mobile home were okay. So Brandon helped his neighbors clear the debris.

Clint was unable to check on his own home until three days after the storm. That's when he saw the devastation. While only there for about thirty minutes, he learned how his wife and step dad had spent three days trying to cut the road so they could get out. When Clint arrived, they still were not out. Clint recalled walking and crawling over and under trees for about a quarter of a mile just to see the house. Clint shared how he was blessed that he needed a new roof, but the structure was in good shape. While there were three pine trees down by his new well, the well was in good shape. He only needed a small amount of fencing replaced.

Clint's father, Virgil spent a great deal of time at the Emergency Operations Center. When Virgil was able to return home, his home was destroyed. Storms following Hurricane Michael dropped more limbs on their home, which did even more damage. Virgil and his wife Karen are still living in a recreational vehicle waiting on the construction of their new home. Clint's grandmother was at Marianna Health and Rehab, where she received excellent care.

Clint admitted, "I experienced difficulties determining which road was which, but knowing the streets was helpful." Landmarks and street signs were gone. "The area around Noland Street was probably the worst as far as damage and fallen trees, and it was very difficult to know where you were," he shared.

Marianna Police Department

As soon as the storm was over the Marianna Police Department started evaluating the situation to see how they could help. The Florida Highway Patrol were staged at Chipola College to respond, but were trapped by fallen trees. That night other troopers arrived with equipment to move huge fallen trees on Jefferson Street, because the City of Marianna did not have equipment large enough to remove them. "The officers were asking for street names, because they didn't know where they were," explained Becky. It's hard to believe one could get lost in a small town of about 6,000 people. Most of us grew up here and knew the place like the back our hands. Yet, the damage was so severe, rescue workers were getting lost due to lack of signage and familiar land marks. "Nothing was identifiable," Becky added. In addition, "it was dark and there were no lights." "We were unable to receive calls," Lieutenant Stroud shared. "People were calling from Texas, New York and everywhere trying to check on family," Becky continued, "and the Sheriff's Department was unable to receive calls, because their phones were down."

Chief Baggett decided to walk home to check on his house, and pick up some batteries. Meanwhile, Marianna Police Officers continued to make their way down City streets. "The year had been really wet prior to the storm," Chief Baggett explained, "which might have been part of the reason for downed trees." Lt. Stroud shared, "we were running over a lot of trees, little trees." He continued, "then, it got to a point where the roads weren't passable." The police force was unable to drive down any road except Lafayette Street (US 90), which was covered in porcelain from transformers.

Sunrise at Madison Street Park after Hurricane
Michael. Photo provided by Chief Baggett.

This led to immediate patching of tires. The police department had a small compressor, and initially were able to obtain patches from the Public Works Department. Then, they were blessed again when O'Reilleys Part Store opened. "We were patching tires in mass," Lieutenant Stroud explained. "Leon County sent one person that night, but the streets were impassable," Stroud reiterated.

Chief Baggett explained, "all the ambulances were staged at the Public Service Building." "There was a man who was cut, and a deputy had to transport him, because ambulances couldn't respond," Hayes continued. "The same night at 2 a.m. a citizen called in a panic and a deputy picked him up and took him to the Public Service Building." "Then Jackson Hospital started transporting patients out, but they were blocked in," Becky explained.

That morning while contemplating what to do next with the City Manager, Chief Baggett took a photo of the sunrise on Madison Street. "I was wondering if we would have any help coming at all – it takes time" Chief Baggett shared.

Lieutenant Tyler Scarborough patching tires. Photo provided by Chief Hayes Baggett.

Davey arrived about three to four days after the storm. Lieutenant Stroud elaborated on how officers brought in chainsaws. "Thank God for Anderson Columbia who were helping to clear Lafayette Street" Chief Baggett added. Then, the police officers noticed Captain Brice Phillips from the Marianna Fire Department operating some equipment from Anderson Columbia to clear the streets. This would help relieve tensions of citizens waiting to be cut out. "The most thankful thing was to drive in the Riverside area and find that no one had died because of the trees and damage was so extreme," Chief Baggett shared. "Not many had evacuated because of lack of time," he continued.

At the station and still in shock, the Marianna Police Department was living off peanut butter, applesauce and butterscotch pudding. The officers were working 16 hour days clearing streets. "We all worked together as a community" Hayes shared. "I'm thankful for the work the churches did in the community," he continued. "People showed up with supplies, and not just big groups, but also individuals." Officers from Largo, Davey, Leon, New York, and Tallahassee showed up and were a big help to the City of Marianna. They stayed in tents and Jackson Hospital fed them. Several local officers lost their homes and despite their own despair, showed to help others in the City. The Police Chief's Association sent supplies. The dispatch center in New Jersey brought Thanksgiving Dinner from Cracker Barrel to the Police Department. "Winn Dixie opened their doors and were very good to the officers," Chief Baggett explained. "Winn Dixie gave the officers groceries" he continued.

Kim Applewhite, Marianna Clerk/Finance Director

"Neighbors helping neighbors, citizens taking their equipment out and helping the fire department to clear roads," Kim continued. Kim explained that this went on for

143

days and weeks. Food was airdropped in because people were desperate. "We had a station set up every day for a good six weeks after the storm, where people could get supplies and a hot meal." she continued. Kim elaborated how people used it every day, because it is a low-income area that lacks the resources and "we needed that stuff," Kim added. "You just don't realize, until you go through something like a category 5 hurricane, what it's like, but it brings out the good in people too," she continued.

Not only was Kim trying to help the people in Grand Ridge, in Marianna she was trying to figure out how to get the Clerk's Office back up and running. "How do we continue to pay our employees who are working 24 hours a day, and get back operational," she shared. Having never encountered this situation, and without Internet services, Kim and her staff were treading in unfamiliar territory. The City was able to obtain hot spots for cellular services. "The banks called and were doing anything they could to help us," she shared. "They even said they'd hand deliver the cash for payroll if we need it," Kim continued. The previous year the City had purchased a new software system and started utilizing "the cloud", which enabled them to access records, they wouldn't have had access to before. "It was expensive software, but it allowed us to keep operating," she shared. "We didn't miss a payroll and vendors continued to get paid."

Clay Wells, Marianna Parks and Recreation Director

The night following the storm Clay Wells walked to town to survey the damage. "It was complete devastation and my initial thoughts was it looked like a nuclear bomb had gone off," Clay explained. He immediately went to work thinking about how they would live the next two or three weeks without electricity and other modern technologies that people take for granted. He patched holes in roofs with his tarps and used some cardboard and tape to secure the broken windows. That night they were all overwhelmed and trying to figure out what their next steps would be.

While Clay and Crystle couldn't drive to town, they were able to drive to the hospital that was less than a mile away. Crystle went to work and Florida State Hospital was in crisis mode. There wasn't enough water on hand. The water at the hospital and the City of Chattahoochee was out. "Governor Rick Scott flew in National Homeland Security Helicopters full of water to Florida State Hospital" Clay shared. Crystle receipted in the water and Clay spent the next two days delivering water to the different units at the hospital free of charge. He explained how the helicopters made five or six trips a day dropping off water in a big field at the institution. They would unload the water off the helicopters onto the big trucks and take it to the warehouse to receipt in before delivering the water to the units of the hospital. During this time Clay, Crystle and their kids were able to stay in her office, where there was air conditioning. They took their grills and refrigerated items with them. Clay cooked on the grills at the hospital for everyone who was working those first couple of days. Others brought food and pitched in with the effort.

On Saturday Jim Dean called and instructed Clay to report on Monday morning to the City of Marianna. That same day Clay loaded his children and mother up and traveled to his sister's home in Atlanta. This is where they would stay during the recovery period. While Clay was traveling to Atlanta, his sister was preparing supplies for him to bring back on his return trip. Clay loaded up his truck with generators, tarps, gas, lights, cords and similar items before returning Sunday morning to prepare his and his neighbors' homes, "so we could figure out how to live," Clay shared.

Monday morning Clay reported to work at the City of Marianna to figure out what needed to be done. "For the first couple of weeks me and my staff reported to the Wastewater Treatment Plant and filled up generators all around town for lift stations, wells and stuff like that," Clay explained. After he got his staff started at the Wastewater Treatment Plant, Monday through Wednesday, Clay and Jeff went out to the Marianna Educational Recreation Expo (M.E.R.E.) to collect and secure items. Clay's office was destroyed. Computers and other items were locked up in a small concession stand. The barn was also destroyed, so they secured the equipment that had been stored there.

Florida Public Utilities

After the storm Mason went outside and every direction from the Emergency Operations Center was blocked with fallen trees. When he contacted the office, he learned that power was out from Jackson County to the coast. "Fernandina was staged with our guys to cut lines wrapped in the trees," Mason explained. "Three guys cut one lane with chainsaws on Panhandle Road to get the Florida Highway Patrol out." Mason went to check on his home, but was unable to get into his subdivision. "I met up with four looters at the shopping center where Hibbetts . . . [Sports] . . . , Roses, Bealls Outlet and Big Lots were located," he continued. "They left, disguising what they were doing by picking up debris." Mason reported the looters.

Mason wanted to go to the Public Service Building at Chipola College where his family was, but couldn't get through town. Mason turned back to take Hwy 71 North and turn west onto Caverns Road. "I saw two cars wrecked with power poles and trees on top of the cars," Mason continued. He stopped to check on the passengers, but did not find anyone inside the vehicles.

Mason called the Florida Department of Transportation and asked them to bring excavators to help the first responders get out where they could help the citizens in need. Mason remembered seeing what looked like hundreds of Florida Highway Patrol cars. By the time he reached his family it was midnight.

Mason, his family and friends slept in the front room of the dorms. His children were with his ex-wife on 4th Street, but were okay. Then, they lost cell services. "The cell towers went down because the generators needed fuel and they couldn't get to them to refuel."

Thursday, Mason returned to the Emergency Operations Center. The backup generator went out. So he picked up a backup generator. After that the linemen went to 20 hours a day for 22 days straight. There were more than 600 linemen hired and paid for by Florida Public Utilities, which included meals, restrooms and vehicles. Some of the workers came from Mississippi, Illinois, Indiana, Central and South Florida, Ohio, Louisiana and Alabama. The Florida Public Utilities Marianna office was the operations base. New York and New Jersey Police Officers were doing wellness checks and Tallahassee Police Officers were providing security to prevent people from looting Florida Public Utilities' supplies at the Ag Center on Highway 90, Eastside Baptist Church, Milk and Honey and other locations. Two of the linemen completely lost their homes.

Florida Public Utilities rented a catering service out of Jacksonville to provide 660 meals, three times a day. On Breaks Mason went home to work. His family was taking care of things at home. "It was a great community effort and for the first few days people were very understandable," Mason remembered. "We had to completely recreate the system from substations out." He remembered how it was very hot and the ground was saturated from the rain. The last to have power were 25 days out. "Florida Public Utilities had a deadline set by the governor and they made the deadline."

"One of our linemen's dad was killed in Chipley," Mason shared. "He was run over by someone not obeying warning signs."

Mason had minor damage at home and his family was back home on the Friday after the storm. "For the first three days I didn't sleep," he continued. "My phone would start ringing at 4 a.m.," he added. "I'm proud of the community, linemen and company."

Jackson Hospital

Kevin Daniel shared that all communications went down at Jackson Hospital for five days. During the last upgrade, the hospital had decided to keep the old generator. No one was able to feel the power failure within the hospital. The State of Florida evacuated 40 patients by ambulances sent from Tennessee to Tallahassee once the hospital went to generator and there was no communications. "When the ambulances arrived, they cut their way in on Interstate 10," he explained. "We never lost air conditioning and the emergency room remained functional," Kevin explained. However, he noted that elective surgery could not be resumed for five days until electricity was restored. During the cleanup after Hurricane Michael, the electricity was on and off. Kevin shared Jackson Hospital lost their warehouse, which will need to be reconstructed. While some of the buildings need to be replaced, "we are still dealing with FEMA and our insurance company," he stated.

During the storm Kevin's family stayed home to weather the storm. They had more than 90 trees down on their property. "I was glad I had already taken down fifteen trees during the summer," Kevin shared. While there was no structural damage to his home, it took 36 hours for the road to be cleared leading to his house.

James Grant, Building Official.

Jimmy Grant, Building Official shared how he immediately

began working toward getting his office operational. Within a week he had completed his first task. Only two days after the storm Jimmy was back at work but was unable to issue permits. "I told people to go ahead and get started and I would get with them later," Jimmy shared. "I could make it out of my road to Hwy 71 and to Hwy 90, but that far," he continued. That didn't slow down the dedicated building official. Within two weeks he was issuing permits 14 – 16 hours seven days a week, except for Sunday morning when he attended church with his wife.

Sergeant Martin Basford, Jackson County Sheriff's office

After the storm was over Martin realized he was trapped with about 30 State Troopers at Chipola College. They immediately started trying to get Fire Rescue out. Martin was able to obtain a key to a front end loader parked near Chipola College. It was owned by Gulf Coast Utility Company, who were working on a Stormwater facility at Chipola College. He began pushing trees out of the road.

"There were lots of people at the Public Service Building and there was no food," Martin explained. Martin shared how he was able to use Chipola College's grill and "Winn Dixie provided a little food." Although they didn't have seasonings, they were very appreciative.

Thursday night Martin attempted to go home and check on his livestock. His children showed cattle with Future Farmers of America and 4-H. When he saw that it was too dangerous, Martin went back to check on his family.

By the time he returned to Chipola College, Martin's family was asleep. He recalled how it was so hot that he slept in his truck. That night Martin learned there was a death in Alford and they needed help getting to Chris Sikes, James and Sikes Funeral Homes owner.

Friday morning Jamie McAllister, Public Service Director at Chipola College and Auxiliary Deputy, joined Martin in using Gulf Coast Utility Company's front end loader to cut a path to Chris Sikes' home. Along the way they were joined by David Johnson, Lance Massengill and Aaron Kincaid, who lived nearby. "It took most of one day to clear to Chris Sikes' home and Tara Estates," Martin shared. Tara Estates is a subdivision located in the same area. While on Angela Drive in Tara Estates, Martin cut a path for Paula Livergood and her mother, who needed ADA access. When he was clearing the road, it was just one lane. Many people begged him to clear their driveways, but he was just trying to get the roadways open. After he cleared the way to Chris Sikes home, he went to his father's home to check on family.

"One day I got overheated and was exhausted, so I sat down to rest" Martin explained. When Martin looked up he saw someone walking through the woods with a granola bar and water for him. "It was humbling because people had no supplies, but brought us refreshments," Martin added. Martin and Jamie teamed up together and used their chainsaws to help clear the roads for days. They opened up driveways, freed people who were trapped, picked up supplies, helped hand out supplies and helped the law enforcement officers' families at Chipola College.

"I was overwhelmed by the number of other agencies that came and stayed in tents, and it's a mile long list," Martin explained.

Ten days after Hurricane Michael came through, Martin and his wife celebrated their 17th anniversary. He treated her to dinner in Dothan. "It was like a vacation to sit in the AC and eat," he shared.

After about two weeks Martin worked at the Emergency Operation Center. When he was off duty, he worked helping others who were trapped. At home he was blessed to have mostly cosmetic damage to his house. However, he lost two barns, fencing, six pecan trees and a field of 17 year old pine trees that he was planning to harvest to pay for his children's college education. He also remembered how the swampy areas stunk.

Martin's family is heavily involved in 4-H and FFA, with Martin holding the position of chairman of the Fed Cattle Show. The Prospect Steer Show check-in was scheduled for October 11th, which had to be cancelled. The Fed Cattle show was scheduled for February. Martin explained that the show in October is at the beginning of the project and the Fed Cattle Show is at the project completion. After the storm the kids did not have feed for their cattle. Martin shared how one girl, Emma Caraway, walked seven miles one way every day to feed her cattle. "Emma had several show calves" Martin continued. Several days after the storm Martin called to check on the 4-H leader and learned that the Caraways couldn't drive to their home. Martin cleared a path for them. "Lots of kids carried water long distances," he added. Emma later won Best Jackson County Raised Steer, which was her goal. After the storm Martin heard a saying repeated many times. "How do you eat an elephant? One bite at a time."

The Florida Cattleman's Association from South Florida helped Martin and others with fencing and transporting cattle, which made a huge difference. A newly formed 4-H club from Newberry, Florida and another club from Gainesville, Florida brought cow food, fencing tools, feeding troughs for cows and horses, and generators. They stayed with the Caraways and helped rebuild fencing. Other 4-H clubs also came to help.

When it was time to have the Fed Cattle Show, the Ag Center was unavailable because other agencies were using it due to being misplaced. Southern Cattle Company allowed the Cattlemen to use their facilities and provided livestock judging and a judge.

Corporal Michael Mears, Jackson County Sheriff's Office

Mike shared that when the storm was over, he went back to his truck. He couldn't drive very far. Mike's friend and his friend's neighbors got some chainsaws and started cutting him a way out. "By the time I got back to Kynesville Highway, I literally had a caravan of cars behind me that were not from this area, but were wanting me to lead them out," Mike continued. "We were driving in people's backyards," he added. "I finally was able to get a bunch of folks out to Highway 231, so they could go check on their families," Mike shared.

Mike began patrolling the area, knocking on doors and checking on people. "By the grace of God, our radio communications were still working," he continued. Mike shared how his cell phone service was sporadic, but worked. Mike worked all night until daylight Thursday. For about four days Mike slept either on the floor in the office or in his vehicle whenever he wasn't on duty. "I didn't even know if I had a home left, because I couldn't get back to my house," he continued. Mike's mother lives with him, but he had evacuated her to a family member's house north of Marianna. "She stayed there during the storm and for a couple of days after until I could find somewhere for us to stay," Mike continued. Just prior to the storm, Mike had brought his mother home from a nursing home. He had been taking care of her since her stroke. "She doesn't understand why our home was destroyed," Mike shared. Mike's wood frame house was built by my grandfather about 140 years ago. Several trees fell on the house. It was standing, but the roof was gone and it had water damage. "Believe it or not, there was a non-profit organization run by retired military and first responders from all over the country called Team Rubicon and they arrived after one of the Captain's at the Sheriff's office gave my name to them," he added. About five days after the storm one of the men from Team Rubicon called Mike and told him they were at his house. "There was a caravan of volunteers with chainsaws and they literally cut my house out from under the trees and they did that in a matter of hours," Mike explained. He explained that the team was very professional and stacked the trees neatly by the road for removal. "These wonderful people work off donations and volunteer their time with people who have been through natural disasters, and I cannot praise them enough," Mike added.

Photos provided by Michael Mears.

Mike worked about two weeks straight. When he had his first break, Mike didn't wake up for 24 hours. He was able to shower but couldn't take a hot shower for a while. Volunteers, local churches and restaurants provided hot meals for the officers for which Mike was thankful. "Jackson Hospital opened up their kitchen to first responders and gave us free meals every day," Mike recalled. "I think everyone was devastated by the storm," Mike shared. "I don't think anything anyone, or City or County could do could've prepared us for the magnitude of a storm like this," Mike added. "One thing I can say is the Jackson County Sherriff's Department was wonderful in helping their deputies and the citizens of this county and I saw it first-hand." Mike shared how in his thirty years of law enforcement experience, he'd never seen an agency come together like they had as an agency and a family.

Photos provided by Michael Mears.

Mike explained that he tried to get assistance from FEMA in tarping his house. "I was declined twice, because I had homeowners insurance," he explained. "All I asked for were tarps" he continued. "I didn't ask for any money." Mike shared "I came home one day and there were tarps on my roof and I don't know who did it." Mike's neighbors wouldn't tell anything

154

except everything was okay. Mike had previously taken the meat out of the freezer and given it to his neighbors to grill and feed their families. While Mike doesn't know for sure, he feels like his neighbors helped him. "I live in a very old part of Marianna and we tend to take care of one another." Mike shared that he feels closer to his neighbors now.

Mike had homeowners and contents insurance that his mother had been paying for more than thirty years. Initially, they only wanted to give him $7000 for the entire house. Mike felt like the company harassed him. According to Mike there were so many claims that the insurance companies had to train and send inexperienced adjusters out. The adjuster that visited Mike's home was there for less than twenty minutes and only took a few photos. Mike had to hire a structural engineer for both of his and his mother's house. The other house was totally destroyed and unlivable too. "The old shot gun house that my mother owned next door literally shifted on its foundation," he explained. The house had been on cinder blocks and the hurricanes moved the house off the blocks. Mike's house had rotated on its foundation about four inches. It took Mike several months to receive the structural engineering reports. Then, he had to hire a public adjuster to help him battle the insurance company. The insurance company's adjuster had mixed up the floors, walls and ceiling in his report. If that wasn't enough, Mike explained that he had to contact the Insurance Commissioner for the State of Florida and file a complaint. Not long after that Mike was able to get a decent check to rebuild his home. The process took nearly a year. His house has now been torn down. He's early in the process of building a new home. Mike's mother is living with his cousin and her husband. Mike is living in his cousin's camper and has been for over a year. Mike explained repeatedly how thankful he is to his cousin and her husband for taking care of him and his mother.

Mike found a contractor out of Gilchrist County to help him rebuild. Mike explained that "the subcontractors are booked out or they think they have found a cash cow and they overprice almost to the point of gouging their own people." "I don't want to say all subcontractors are price gouging," Mike explained. "It's just a select few." "We've had people coming from out of this area and they have tried so hard to rip us off in this County," Mike continued. "You just can't do people that way that have been devastated the way we have," he added. They have taken advantage of people who are living in a desperate state.

Sheriff Lou Roberts, and Governor Rick Scott work hand in hand with Corporal Michael Mears in rebuilding the community. Photo provided by Michael Mears.

Wilanne Daniels

When Wilanne arrived at the Emergency Operations Center that Thursday, things were just getting started. She hadn't missed much. "The first several days, it was neighbors helping neighbors," she clarified. "That's something FEMA says 'the first

72 hours are on you,'" she continued. This simply means that it takes time to deploy all the efforts taking place.

After checking in, Wilanne and her family ventured out to their home in Alford to see how it had survived and gather up clothes and supplies so that they could continue stay with her husband's family in town. This would allow her to be close to the work of overseeing recovery. Both her home and mother-in law's homes were fine. "Our home in Alford had a spot that leaked during a normal rain storm, but after Hurricane Michael there was not a drop of water," she shared. "Just a total miracle!" They did have to get a new roof, but she was thankful the house was standing and dry. "I really, truly believe in my heart that God knew and spared me, because of what I was going to have to face with the County and the need for me to be able to focus on helping others," she elaborated. "If we had lost our house it would have been very difficult," she added. While out they picked up a generator from her house and took it to her parents. While she was out, she was observing damage and strike teams arriving.

Except for at night, she was at the Emergency Operations Center dealing with issues. She explained how debris contractors began rolling into town starting the day after the storm. They began along with locals pushing debris off the road. Once the contractors arrived they started systematically clearing every single road. There was a map in the EOC and every day cleared roads would be marked off. Jackson County is large in area and has over 900 miles of dirt, over 700 miles of paved, and over 200 miles of private roads, requiring a coordinated effort.

Incident Management Team from Virginia Beach, Virginia. The lady with blue jacket in the middle of the photos Carley Schwartz from Florida Department of Emergency Management. Photo provided by Wilanne Daniels.

On Friday an Incident Management Team, which is a team with a mutual aid agreement with the State of Florida deployed during emergencies, arrived from Virginia Beach, Virginia. According to Wilanne the team had an incident commander and different team members assigned to help with every part of the recovery group, such as finance, safety, public information officer and similar types support help. "They basically come in and run your Emergency Operations Center, when a community is so devastated that their own people cannot adequately do it," she explained. "In our case, we had people trapped, who couldn't get to the Emergency Operations Center, who would normally do these functions" she clarified. There were other circumstances where people had evacuated and could not get back in. The community is still in charge while the incident management team is there, but they provide the needed support. "They were the greatest blessing that you can even imagine!" They were able to coordinate the FEMA urban search and rescue, which went door-to-door to every single home in our entire County to ensure they were alive and not trapped or in need of medical attention. The Public Information Officer coordinated with Jackson County's Public Information Officer to ensure she could provide information as quickly and accurately as possible, which was challenging because of the isolation experienced. "I really believe God sent every last person that was supposed to be here to help guide and shape the way!" The Incident Management Team was here about two weeks. Carley Shwartz, from the Tallahassee Department of Emergency Management, was sent to be a liaison between Jackson County and the State of Florida. "She really stepped up, pitched in anywhere she possibly could or was needed," Wilanne shared. "They are my heroes!"

Left: Red Cross Worker whose name is Marianna. Wilanne remembered saying "Marianna came to save Marianna". **Right**: Red Cross worker from Nicaragua, who now lives in Miami, with Jackson County Administrator, Wilanne Daniels. Wilanne and Ryan made a connection with him because Ryan has been to Nicaragua three times. Photos provided by Wilanne Daniels

Just a few days after Hurricane Michael came through Marianna, questions began arising about when Jackson County employees would return to work. It was decided that the beginning of the following week, Jackson County employees would return to work with the clear understanding that everyone needed flexibility, which helped people to return to some normalcy. During this time Wilanne remembers the Board of County Commissioner meetings taking place two or more times a week at City Hall in Marianna. The Jackson County offices received damage and they didn't have a generator. Their offices were scattered about the County. The administration offices were relocated to the Jackson County Health Department Building.

"Many of the early meetings stemmed from Jackson County not having a disaster contract or a monitoring firm named in a contract," Wilanne recalled. In fact, in one of the meetings a conversation came up about the debris company's inability to continue without a monitor in place. The County would be required to go through the procurement process. Due to issues relating to the procurement not qualifying as an emergency purchase, the result was the State deciding that all physically constrained Counties would have debris contracts run by the Florida Department of Transportation. "This turned out to be a blessing with the Florida Department of Transportation to date spending about $110 million dollars on our behalf for debris removal" she shared. According to Wilanne, the County's conclusion of the debris removal will be about $10 million. Wilanne shared that the arrangement was sometimes challenging because   there   were   no   clear

Left: County Administrator Wilanne Daniels with Governor Rick Scott. **Right:** County Administrator Wilanne Daniels with her newborn Lydia and Senator Marco Rubio taken in the City Commission Chambers at Marianna City Hall. Photos provided by Wilanne Daniels.

160

guidelines about who was responsible for what.

Friday after the storm the Jackson County Jail's generator went out. No stores were open. Wilanne's husband, Ryan, is a mechanic. He climbed on the roof, diagnosed the problem, and called a connection with an Auto Parts Store. He repaired the generator for free to help Jackson County. During the same time frame, there was a post on social media about a couple who was trapped and only had enough formula for one bottle for their baby. Ryan went on a mission to find formula and whatever else the couple needed. According to Wilanne, Ryan went into Winn Dixie as they were closing the doors and insisted on buying formula before they closed to help the family. At the same time Wilanne had Jackson County Road and Bridge out clearing the road so Ryan could get the formula to the baby.

Left: Member of National Guard from near Saint Augustine holding newborn baby Lydia. **Right:** Sheriff Lou Roberts meeting with Governor Rick Scott. Photos provided by Wilanne Daniels.

Wilanne's giving heart does not fall far from her family tree. Her father almost made a business out of helping neighbors and connecting others with relief free of charge following the storm. Meanwhile, Wilanne's mother was taking care of the children, so the entire family could help in the community. Ryan also comes from a giving family. His parents have a hunting lodge, which they have allowed many volunteers to stay at free of charge over the past year. They also rented it out to a few people here to make money, but always at a reasonable rate.

Urban Search and Rescue meetings. Photos provided by Wilanne Daniels

As disaster responses were underway, help arrived. Other cities all over the country sent first responders. Organizations most in this area had never heard of arrived with semis of supplies to assist the town. In the meanwhile, one of the best things that happened was people began to return to their normal routines despite their own personal losses and devastation. They found a new normal in helping one another.

Chapter Seven
Business Discoveries

*Marianna – Recovering Hearts Welcome
Your Holiday Business*

Kay Dennis

On October 10th, 2018 at 2:00 pm the City of Marianna changed forever. Buildings standing firm and tall for centuries were suddenly empty doll-house structures. Monuments honoring military veterans and fallen war heroes were instantly demolished. Every street in town and most homes were covered with huge trees. Communication stopped immediately. Citizens and visitors lost cellular, land line, television and Internet connections. Being approximately seventy miles inland, most locals had lived through many hurricanes. The very worst storms remembered had some wind, random tornadoes and rain. Hurricane Michael would defy the odds and make landfall so quickly that no one was prepared. Citizens cleaned off the shelves of the local stores the night before, but most only had supplies that would last a couple of days, which would be more than was usually needed. The four to six hour period the eye wall passed over Marianna looked like a blizzard. Seeing past the end of one's arm was nearly impossible, due to the whiteout conditions. Many ventured out during the middle of the eye only to find the worst of the storm was yet to come. Assistance would only be available after streets were cleared. Two days following the storm, purchasing fuel for a generator meant paying cash and traveling 60 miles or more through dangerous pig-trails of fallen power poles and trees.

How could a small rural town possibly recover from the physical and mental effects of Hurricane Michael? Almost immediately fire and police officers from around the country arrived to assist locals and keep citizens safe. Utility and road crews from everywhere imaginable began helping to clean-up and restore electrical services nonstop around the clock. Neighbors helped neighbors recover family and friends trapped within their homes. First responders were sent out as areas became clear. People from all types of relief organizations brought food, clothing, and other supplies to the needy. The community rallied and continue to rally together to help one another, all thankful to have survived Hurricane Michael.

A little over a month later Marianna continues to heal, but hope floats all around. Businesses are beginning to open. "Our roof is open in the back and front, and we have mortar damage," explained Desiree Baggett, owner of A Wild Hair, "but last week we had a large turnout for a holiday sale called Holly Jolly." "My fuel pumps and awnings were completely destroyed," detailed Mohammed Shahjahan, new owner of Adnam Food Mart, "but the convenience store is open and busy." Maranda Hartman, new owner of the Waffle Iron clarified how she had lost the entire dining room of her restaurant, "but since the kitchen was untouched we setup tents with heaters behind the building for a temporary dining area until after Christmas." Maranda also told how she was thankful for the birth of her first grandson, Eli, the night before Hurricane Michael arrived. Luke Shores, owner of Cobb

Front-End and Cobb's 2 shared how their business was closed approximately two weeks and today Internet services had finally been restored enabling the business to process credit cards. "We have been blessed and prayers have been answered that business is returning," Luke stated. Gus and Fran Peace are awaiting repairs at Gus No Fuss Pool Service, "but we boarded up the windows and went back to work," stated Fran. Sissy Woodall owner of Living Life Repurposed shared how she had quite a bit of damage, but another business, Lemon Squeeze, was allowing her to display seven Christmas trees to sell special Christmas ornaments until her building could be repaired in 2019. Terry Owens was glad to describe that a portion of the roof would need replacing, but two weeks ago they had begun opening one room at a time in his gallery of eclectic collections. Suzanne Owens, manager of Be Spoken expressed how one window was boarded up, but the other was full of Christmas displays to provide hope for the community. Art and Michele Tabor Kimbrough, shared how the roof was removed from Michele's studio and placed atop the Art Factory Gallery, but the gallery would be open by appointment only during the holidays. Finally, Chuck Smith, owner of Smith and Smith Jewelers was pleased to tell that he was already working on some customized Christmas and hurricane jewelry designs.

Much like a classic children's story, the citizens whether tall or small are singing and preparing for Christmas. As it turns out, it's not the things in the world that mean the most, but the hearts of those who share their all. Come visit Marianna and support the recovery.[3] [4]

N‌ot only were the residents' lives turned upside down by the storm, but the businesses that are the heart of Marianna struggled to stay alive, pay their employees and provide goods and services to the community. Some would recover quickly. Other businesses would require months. Still others would never recover. More than a year after the storm some businesses are in operation in substandard conditions.

Mowrey Elevator Company after Hurricane Michael. Photo provided by Lori Nable.

---

[3] From "Marianna: Recovering Hearts Welcome Your Holiday Business," by Kay K. Dennis, 24 November 2018, *Tallahassee Democrat.*

[4] From "Marianna: Recovering Hearts Welcome Your Holiday Business," by Kay K. Dennis, 27 November 2018, *Tallahassee Democrat.*

Photos provided by Rhonda Dykes.

Photos provided by Lori Nable.

Photos provided by Scott Hagan.

Photos provided by Scott Hagan.

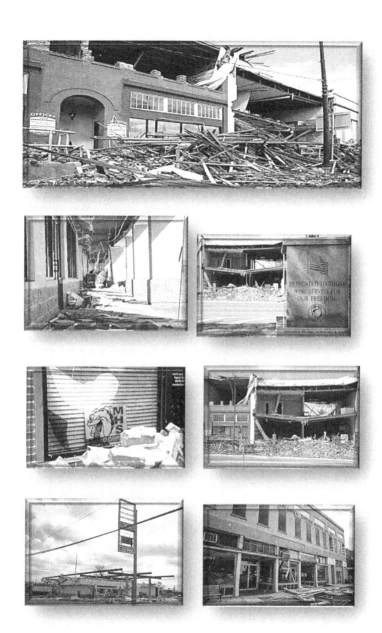

Photos provided by Scott Hagan.

Photos provided by Scott Hagan.

Photos provided by Rhonda Dykes.

Photos provided by Rhonda Dykes.

Florida Showcase Realty

After Hurricane Michael stormed through Marianna, Ann Jones and her family were in a state of panic. Her son's work prevented him from being able to leave and check on the family. "We had no Internet or cell phones and I felt isolated," she explained. "We went into survival mode and I don't know how many days we were like that," Ann shared. The family had a generator, food and water. It would be days before anyone could get to them. "We were okay in the house and we never left," she added. Finally, she saw her son walking down the road with a chainsaw and axe, and knew hope was on the way.

"I didn't realize how bad thing were, but I was thankful," she shared. Ann's daughter-in-law, who is a hospice nurse, climbed through mounds of debris to help others. At this point the family went into help-mode. Ann's pastor, Kevin Yoder called and sent some Mennonites, who had just arrived in town, to help her.

"An arborist from Virginia called on the road to my house," she explained. Ann didn't know anything about the man, but he would be a blessing in the days to come. "He stood in front of the house for 45 minutes and prayed," she continued. "Then, he said 'God sent me.'" Ann allowed the arborist to stay at her home, while he helped her and others in the community.

"There was a huge power cable down in my driveway, and we didn't know if it was live," Ann described. "I noticed it was fraying and was broke," she added. "It could have cut someone in two." Once the family knew the cable wasn't live, they were able to get equipment in to remove the tree off her house.

An orthopedic doctor that Ann's son worked for bought in approximately 15 Boston Butts. Ann's brother brought buns and Ann's son and someone else brought in grills. "We made about 200 sandwiches and passed them out to the linemen and other

175

workers," she continued. One lineman was so pleased. He shared with Ann that all he had eaten in days was a small bag of chips.

"God sent the Mennonites to distract me," Ann added. They stayed with Ann in her spare bedroom until March or April. Then, they brought campers and showers and setup behind her Florida Showcase Realty office. "Many slept on my office floor," she continued. The electricity was out fourteen days at Ann's office and 28 days at her home. During this time Ann shared "we had the opportunity to help so many people".

Hancock Whitney

Thursday Georgeann loaded up the kids and attempted to drive to town dodging trees and power lines. "When I turned onto Hwy 90 I recognized Bryan Craven and his daughter hitchhiking from Indian Springs," she expressed. "We dropped them off at the Chipola College Baseball field." Then, Georgeann checked on her family. "Everyone was safe but it looked like a bomb had went off," she shared. "I was unable to get to my house, because so many trees were down in the driveway that I couldn't see it," she continued. "I walked through the woods and climbed over downed trees to find my roof totally off and lots of water damage," Georgeann recalled. "You could see daylight through the tongue and groove wood ceiling." Georgeann was in shock. Four days after the storm it took heavy equipment to clear her driveway. "Our clothes were ruined," she stated. "I lost my baby book and photographs," she remembered. So, Georgeann had to temporarily move in with her uncle and grandfather.

As if Hurricane Michael wasn't enough grief for Georgeann's family, her grandfather died on November 28th. "The storm took a toll on him," she recalled. "We couldn't even have a funeral procession because the roads still weren't clear enough."

Coworkers and management from other areas arrived the day after the storm with supplies for Georgeann's staff and to assist with opening the Hancock Whitney Bank in Marianna on

Friday. "We didn't have power, so we let a few people in at a time and there were security guards there from other areas," Georgeann explained. "We began cashing checks up to a limit for anybody." There wasn't much damage to the building and the grounds were cleaned up quickly on Thursday. "Every day, other area . . . [Hancock Whitney] . . . bank workers brought in food for the community, including chicken, hamburgers, hotdogs, drinks and snacks," she shared. "For employees they sent in a fuel truck two to three times a week for automobile and generator fueling, offered zero percent interest loans for five years, gave out grant money and gift cards," she shared. "My friend, Jessica Smith Pensky, who lives away, came with generators for my family and donated gift cards and supplies out of a U-Haul truck." "We worked with one laptop with Internet, no phones, no cell phones and no power for seven days," she continued.

"My uncle's home was without power for 21 days," Georgeann added. Halloween was cancelled in Marianna, so Hancock Whitney gave the workers Halloween candy. "We had a generator, lights, hot water and sewer," she remembered. "I was thankful for Winn Dixie," she shared. Like most people, Georgeann and her family adjusted to the new lifestyle over the weeks to follow.

Elizabeth Simpson

When Hurricane Michael struck, Elizabeth's daughters began calling. Trees hit her home from north to south, and from east to west. Wisconsin and New York Fire Fighters showed up at her door soon after and helped Elizabeth pack up belongings. Meanwhile, her daughter Kathryn flew in from Colorado. Kathryn helped deliver food with Evangel Worship Center. A bedroom in their home was okay, so their daughter Gabrielle helped to remodel it.

Elizabeth Simpson explained "people here are strong." While she noted many evacuated, the ones who remained did not know where to or how to find help. "There was lots to give away but people didn't know where it was," she added. "People came from everywhere to help us move furnishing out of areas of our home that had been flooded," Elizabeth continued. She explained how her daughters had arranged for volunteers and an insurance adjuster to be at her home after the storm.

Elizabeth needed the help with John suffering from lung, esophageal and bone cancer. "Many local people came out and visited John and offered help," she continued. "We had more than 40 trees down in our backyard and an attorney friend and his family from Tallahassee came over, brought some good bagels and helped cleanup our yard," she added gratefully. Her family lived in a FEMA trailer for four months. Elizabeth's mother owned a beach house in Mexico Beach and the roof had been torn off. Her mother's home in town had a great deal of water damage, so she moved in with Elizabeth.

The second floor wall of Elizabeth's office was completely blown out. So, she couldn't open her office, but still looked out for her employees. She learned that Milton's Mini-Storage on Highway 90 West needed someone to help cleanup and rent units after the storm. Elizabeth helped her legal secretary get this job until she reopened the office. The legal secretary was grateful and her family helped Elizabeth during this time. The temperature was extremely hot, but Elizabeth's other secretary gladly accepted a job from a tree cutting service that Elizabeth was able to help her obtain. This enabled the lady to feed and care for her two small children, while she was trying to move back into her home. She also helped Elizabeth by picking up debris in the yard. "It was neighbor helping neighbor," she recalled.

At first Elizabeth used her husband's law office. Court was suspended, because there was no electricity or phone service. When court resumed it was held at the jail, a building on Clinton Street, and the Ag Center on Highway 90. A year out Elizabeth and her staff are in her office, but are still using buckets, and the bathroom has a skylight by way of a hole in the roof. The east wall withstood the storm, but the west wall did not. Elizabeth is planning a mural for the east wall in the future.

Elizabeth Simpson's office after Hurricane Michael. Photo provided by Scott Hagan.

Elizabeth's husband, John went into the hospital in April, and sadly did not survive. However, Elizabeth loves the community and has no plans to leave.

WJAQ FM

After Hurricane Michael made its way through Marianna, WJAQ station owner Steven McGowen made his way to Marianna. Just prior to the storm Steven had purchased a new office and renovated it for the business. What he would find after the storm was more damage than he had anticipated. Hurricane Michael had taken out the electrical power, computers, and furniture. Steve wanted to get the station back on the air as soon as possible to provide much needed information to the area residents and business owners. Steve met with Jeff Sallaway, WJAQ engineer and the managers at Century Link, who allowed the station to relocate temporarily. Betty Demmon showed up at work as quickly as possible, so she could help area residents. .

Possibly because Jackson County is not a large population center, Betty would notice that larger radio station's failed to talk about the rural areas. For this and many other reasons, the community appreciated the efforts of the team at WJAQ FM. They were a lifeline to what was happening in the area and where locals could go to receive assistance.

Photos provided by Betty Demmon.

Not only was the station's office damaged, but the City's tower, that the station had leased space on, was damaged. It would be months before the station became fully operational and had a new tower. Carol Lambes remembered how Steven was willing to write off the bills of their clients that were unable to pay the first month after the storm. Despite the challenges of no equipment, furniture, and computers, the team placed the community as their top priority.

Jim's Buffet and Grill

Maria Andromidas, owner and manager of Jim's Buffet and Grill had damage at the restaurant, as well as at her home. When the doors are not open in a restaurant, money is not being made to pay the bills. This trickles down to employees, who need money to pay their bills and repair their homes. It also hurt people from outside the community, who needed to be able to meet. Marianna was blessed to see Jim's Buffet and Grill open on day twelve following Hurricane Michael. Maria loves Marianna. To give back to the community, she stayed open on Thanksgiving and Christmas to provide a place for people to have a warm meal and celebrate being alive.

Merle Norman

Merle Norman in Marianna is owned by Scott and Ginger Harris. They were thankful to have only minor damages at their store. However, even minor damage is something that requires time and money. The structure had water damage on the east side of the building from where the wind pounded on the roof and side of the establishment. While their damage may sound minor compared to some, Merle Norman in Marianna was closed for fourteen days. Yet, the couple explained that the closure was also due to lack of Internet service and electricity. Some of the repairs they were able to make with the assistance of the Marianna Main Street.

Spears Cafe'

Coe Spears and his wife Loretta Spears love Marianna. Together, they opened a café in a nostalgic and historic building on Orange Street in their retirement years. After Hurricane Michael came through Marianna, the café had some roof and internal damage, but had survived. Coe and Loretta took advantage of the opportunity to help provide food and supplies to the community following the storm.

Waffle Iron after Hurricane Michael. Photos provided by Scott Hagan.

J. Philip Tyler, CPA, LLC

Philip Tyler's business is located in the 1812 House in downtown Marianna. Although the roof had to be replaced, the historic building faired well during the storm. Philip and Kay Tyler lost more than 70 trees, fencing, a boathouse and boat at their home. However, the week following Hurricane Michael, they were pleased to welcome two new grandsons born into their family.

Pinello's Italian Cuisine

Bryan Penello moved to Marianna in 2013 to work for Mark Panichella at Madison's Restaurant. Mark was not only a restaurant owner, but a culinary instructor at Chipola College. So, he was able to convince Bryan to finish his studies. After his 2016 graduation, Bryan and his parents, Arty and Paula, began planning to open an Italian restaurant in Marianna.

During this time Bryan had also fallen in love with Cheyenne Raines. The couple began planning their wedding for October 27, 2018. When Hurricane Michael arrived, Bryan and Cheyenne had already ordered reception napkins and accessories with their wedding date engraved. The date was even embroidered on Bryan's tuxedo.

After the storm the family had some damage in their new restaurant that would slow the opening. Their electrical power wasn't restored at home until October 27th, the date of the wedding. So, Bryan and Cheyenne delayed their wedding until January 19, 2019.

Photo provided by Lori Nable.

Windham Shoe Shop

Dennis Creamer has been the owner of Windham Shoe Shop for the last 25 years and lived in the area for more than 65 years. Dennis explained how he had helped with recovery when Hurricane Andrew struck Homestead, Florida in 1992. However, Dennis shared that Hurricane Michael was the worst storm he had ever seen. One of the differences Dennis noticed was the width and strength of Hurricane Michael. As a result Windham Shoe Shop's street-front window was blown out. He had roof damage and his awnings were damaged. Thankful the items within his shop were not destroyed, Dennis opened his shop without electricity to repair shoes of first responders, linemen and other workers.

Wells Fargo

Jackie Kendall, Marianna Branch Manager, shared "Hurricane Michael was one of the most intense hurricanes to make landfall in our area." Once it was over Jackie and her staff were forced to make decisions regarding the care of their customers. The branch had total interior loss. "Its's been a long year of rebuilding and we had to be creative looking for resources to remain open so we could support our customers and the community," she explained. The construction is now complete

Below: Michael's Toggery after Hurricane Michael. The owner decided to close the store after the storm. Photo photos provided Scott Hagan.

James and Sikes

"Everyone at the funeral home had damage at home," Chris explained. "We had more than 250 trees down at our home, but we were not in a critically affected area." The Florida Independent Funeral Directors' Association helped Chris and his staff numerous times. "They provided 900 gallons of gas and diesel fuel, food, bottled water, hygiene items and staples," he explained. "Plus they checked on us." "The same organization helped Adams Funeral Home in Blountstown, and our sister funeral home in Graceville." "We saw lots of examples of neighbors helping neighbors, especially at first," Chris shared. "After two weeks we saw outside groups coming in with one of the most impressive being Convoy of Hope, who brought in 35 to 40 semi-trailers," he continued. "The Church of Jesus Christ of Latter Day Saints were also very helpful." "We noted armies of tents between the church and the Chipola College Health Center," Chris added.

Chris Sikes, owner and manager of James and Sikes Funeral Home, had been very busy preparing families and bodies prior to Hurricane Michael that they had little time to prepare for the hurricane. After the storm he was trapped at his home. At daylight the following day a team showed up to help cut him out. Multiple bodies were in the funeral home before the storm, and following the storm the business was without electricity for six or seven days. On request Florida Public Utilities brought in a generator on a double-axel trailer. "Within six to eight days we had sixteen deaths, not all storm related, stored here," he shared. Prior to the storm the funeral home had three to four casketed bodies awaiting services, which had to be postponed for two weeks. "The hardest part was the families needed to grieve and couldn't," Chris explained. "They needed to facilitate grief by having the funeral and couldn't." "It was very hard observing," he added. "The Marianna Fire Department helped on a couple occasions." Chris felt blessed that the funeral home facility didn't have major damage and they were able to keep it cool. However, Pinecrest Memorial Gardens had a great deal of storm damage. The mausoleum was destroyed, but the casketed crypts and urns were never compromised. The office had a great deal of damage and the storage building was destroyed.

Photo provided by Rhonda Dykes.

PanCare Health

Photo provided by Kay Dennis.

After Hurricane Michael struck Marianna, Ashley Kelly, Marketing Coordinator for PanCare Health was notified that the Marianna clinic received the most damage of all their clinics. With a goal of eliminating barriers to health care, she quickly went to work ensuring a temporary clinic was available. Ashley explained that during the first few weeks after the storm, their team was seeing at least twenty people every day. The temporary setup, which is still in use, is a huge tent that provided a sterile space for dental, behavioral, primary and urgent health needs.

State Farm

State Farm Independent Contractor, Linda Pforte shared how about 400 catastrophic adjusters noted how the damage caused by Hurricane Michael was different from other hurricanes, because of the number of fallen trees. The windows blew out of Linda's office resulting in a disaster inside. Despite the damage and lack of power and phone service for 28 days, she opened two days after the storm to help the community. This included helping a client that was trapped in her bathroom for three days by a fallen tree.

Lambe's Welding

Doyle Green, owner of Lambe's Welding discovered extensive damage when he returned to his shop. The building Doyle rented for his business was completely destroyed. He lost $250 thousand in inventory that was within the building and $800 thousand in pine trees at another location. Without a building for operations, Doyle is working in two locations: temporary portable buildings where the business was once housed; and an office about a quarter of a mile down the street. Rebuilding is not planned at this time.

The Art Factory

Photo provided by Lori Nable.

Photos provided by Michelle Tabor Kimbrough.

Local artist Michelle Tabor Kimbrough and her husband Art Kimbrough own the Art Factory in downtown Marianna. The

190

building known for the beautiful orange awning provided framing services downstairs and art classes upstairs. Art also had an office upstairs. Michelle rented the upstairs space of the Edward Jones building on the corner for her studio and storage.

After Hurricane Michael Michelle's art desk was seen dangling precariously for weeks. Michelle lost about 80 percent of her storage in the studio. "Most of our damage in our building is our roof, walls, floors that still is not repaired since the parapet walls must be repaired first before the roof can be replaced," she explained. "Every time it rains outside, it rains inside."

Michelle moved her studio into their home, which also received significant damaged. The Art Factory is closed for now. Michelle hopes to reopen by summer 2020 with a new name – "Art Factory Gallery." She will no longer offer framing services. Instead she will have a gallery that opens for exhibits. Meanwhile, her art is available on the Internet.

Living Life Repurposed

Business owners Todd and Sissie Woodall endured major damage at their relatively new business, Living Life Repurposed. Not only was the roof torn away, but the merchandise within the store was ruined. Another business, Lemon Squeeze, allowed the couple to display merchandise in their store until the Woodalls could make repairs. Several months later, the owners would reopen their store.

Accentria

Acentria began preparing before Hurricane Michael arrived. The company provided support to their clients before and after the storm. For nearly a month the office was every day focusing on the needs of their clients. When they weren't helping clients with claims, they were providing food, water, fuel, ice and other resources. All the while the business was operating out of a portable office setup in a Fifth Wheel Recreational Vehicle. They would stay in the portable office for more than four months.

Top Right: Accentria staff and Governor Rick Scott. Photos provided by Accentria.

Photo provided by Nick Rickman, award winning chef and owner of the Salt Block Restaurant.

While businesses fought to stay open, local churches were trying to assist. The primary problem was the local nonprofits and churches were dealing with their own disaster issues. They were helping others, when their own buildings were damaged and supplies were low. Despite the setbacks they were facing, churches and nonprofits put personal concerns aside, and kept moving forward focused on helping others.

Chapter Eight
Others

Traditionally, local nonprofits and churches have been known for helping the disadvantaged or people who were simply down on their luck in the community. While it may only be a little food from their food pantry, or some fuel for a car, the efforts provided by these organizations have always been appreciated.

In the aftermath of Hurricane Michael not only were these organizations hurting, but the community needs were more expensive. Each group would take time to search out ways to help those who needed it most. Much like the first responders and government officials, churches and nonprofit organizations put the needs of the community ahead of their own.

Historic Saint Luke's Episcopal Church on Lafayette Street in Marianna after Hurricane Michael. Photo provided by Father David Green

Saint Luke's Episcopal Church

Father David recalled the day following Hurricane Michael, neighbors and other people brought out their chainsaws and made a path out of their neighborhood. Although it wasn't easy to maneuver between the stacks of downed trees, they were able to leave. His first planned stop was to check on Saint Luke's Episcopal Church located downtown. "The damage I saw driving the six miles from my house to Saint Luke's was incredible!" he recalled.

At the church Father David inspected the three buildings. He noticed a faucet running outside, which was not good. "It was very dark in the undercroft downstairs and I couldn't see much, but I could tell the carpet was wet," he explained. "I went upstairs in this beautiful American-Gothic house of worship and felt really blessed all the stain glass windows were still intact." "I looked around and noticed the doors were secure and the windows were sound, but there were leaves all over the carpet," he detailed. He couldn't figure out how all the leaves got in, but proceeded to take photos with his cell phone. Then, he communicated with the Diocese of the Central Gulf Coast through their emergency system, though all communication was spotty. Father David and Charlotte's children, who lived away, had been watching the news reports and were worried. Within the next couple of days, despite spotty cellular signals, they were able to make contact through texting.

Father Steve Banes from Holy Nativity in Panama City had evacuated and was trying to return home. Bishop Russell Kendrick, the diocese Administrator, Dwight Babcock, and Father Banes came through Marianna on Friday and saw the devastation. Father Banes would later find Holy Nativity Episcopal School was destroyed.

The Bishop's annual visit was scheduled for that Sunday following the storm and there was discussion about whether there would be a service. The church building was not an option because of the lighting. The parish hall was in relatively good shape and had natural lighting with large windows. So, they decided to move services to the Parish Hall for that Sunday, especially since there were four people scheduled for confirmation into the Episcopal Church.

The very next day a team from Christ Church in Pensacola, including the priest and three men with chainsaws, cleaned up enough trees in the driveway and parking lot to allow parking and traffic flow, so a service could take place on Sunday. "They did an amazing job and we couldn't have done it without them," Father David explained appreciatively. "They were absolute heroes!" Not only did they remove the trees out of the driveway, there was a huge metal awning with a canvas covering that had been blown down and was blocking the way into the Parish Hall. The team was able to move the awning out of the way with chains and a tractor.

That Sunday morning there were about 40 people in attendance. "You could definitely feel the presence of God that day," Father David shared. Everyone had been through an ordeal, and most were in shock.

Historic Saint Luke's Episcopal Church after Hurricane Michael. Photo provided by Father David Green.

Many did not know, but Charlotte Green had been having some health issues and using a heart monitor when Hurricane Michael came through Marianna. She was unable to charge the monitor after electrical power was lost. Following Bishop Kendrick's visit, Father David loaded up his wife and dog, and took them to their family home in Gulf Shores. There she was able

198

to recover with air conditioning and electricity. Meanwhile, he was going back and forth between Marianna and Gulf Shores. About sixteen days after Hurricane Michael made landfall, Father David's power was restored at the church and at his home. Then, he brought Charlotte and their dog back home.

Once the power was restored, everyone was excited to worship in the church. The mitigation team had dehumidifiers in the church, but the parish was able to worship in the church until the end of the year. As the mitigation team cleaned, they realized that the church needed to be empty so they could do more work. Unfortunately, the parish has not been able to return worship services to the church building to date. The Parish hall was setup for worship and the congregation adjusted to the new arrangements.

"We received a lot of help from other parishes in the Diocese," Father David shared. "Multiple times Saint Jude's in Niceville came over with crews: Nativity in Dothan came over with workers, generators and supplies; Holy Spirit in Gulf Shores sent money for gift cards; and Saint Paul's in Mobile sent supplies and generators," he explained.

Saint James AME

Prior to the landfall of Hurricane Michael, Reverend Mizer had gone to the bank for cash, which turned out to be a good idea, because the Internet was unavailable afterwards. This meant that cash purchases were the only purchases to be made. However, cash was no good with roads blocked. Without power, keeping food cool was a challenge. "After the first half day without electricity, I noticed people walking around in a daze," Reverend Mizer recalled. "We were without electricity for nine days with no generator," he added. "Then, a member, whose father had a generator, brought it to us for our home." "Our kin folk brought coolers of ice, chicken and water," he continued. "We couldn't have church the following Sunday, so we began making plans to have church services the next Sunday in the church parking lot." Reverend Mizer remembered how during this time the temperatures were unbearably hot, especially for people accustomed to air-conditioning. "People started coming in from everywhere," he continued, "staging at the church." "Locals helped make a path." "Then, we had a big cookout with freezer items," Reverend Mizer shared with a smile.

On Thursday or Friday of the following week electrical power was beginning to be restored in Reverend Mizer's neighborhood. "On Saturday people came and cleaned up the parking lot, but we were able to have church services inside on Sunday," he continued. While there was roof damage, Reverend Mizer recalled no dampness in the air. "We had a church conference call and the denomination announced that they were bringing supplies from Tampa, Orlando, and Miami." "About 50 trucks arrived," he continued. "Boy scouts from Dothan cleared paths for trucks from New York, Philadelphia and Texas led by Judy Mount from the Florida House of Representatives Democratic Office," he shared. "We became a distribution center for two weeks." Judy Mount had learned that supplies were not making it to the neighborhoods on the west side of Marianna. Reverend Mizer made contact with Kevin Yoder, who sent the boy scouts, and Convoy of Hope, with water, and cases of hamburgers and hotdogs. "Judy Mount sent 500 pounds of frozen ribs and we had a community cookout," he shared. "What we were unable to cook, we gave to Spears Café to give away at no cost." "Approximately 3000 folks came through Saint James AME to receive new shirts, suits and shoes from Men's Warehouse," he continued. This was important because many people had lost everything in the storm, and those who had not, were unable to wash their clothes without electricity. "We tried to make sure everyone had something," Reverend Mizer shared.

The weekend of November 10th, 2018, Reverend Mizer traveled to Orlando for a meeting. While he was away he learned that mold and mildew had been discovered in his church and the parsonage. "They came in with Hazmat suits and said we had to leave," he explained. "When we returned home, we had no place to stay." A local hotel allowed the couple to stay a few days for $89 a night. Then, they went about 50 miles away and lodged at a Motel 6. After staying there a month, friends gave them donations for a hotel next door to an Outback restaurant in Dothan. "We had applied for FEMA money, but they only provided $1020 for six months of housing" he shared. "Different churches gave us donations and FEMA gave us another $1012 for property damage," he continued. "We were able to get food stamps from the SNAP program, but after a while it was too many hoops and too much frustration," he shared sadly.

In December, they moved in with their daughter, who lived across the street. "We hired a public adjuster and an attorney for the church and parsonage," he continued. In August 2019 Reverend Mizer's insurance and denomination had provided enough money for the parsonage and the couple was hoping to be in the parsonage by September. However, at the beginning of November 2019 Reverend Mizer and his wife were still unable to move home.

As far as the church goes, Reverend Mizer explained "we have enough money to work on the basement." "The public adjuster quoted $498,000 for both buildings, but we have only received $207,000." The members of the church do not want another mortgage or Small Business Administration loan. So, like several churches, they are sharing another building. Different congregations are allowed time to conduct their services and they juggle use of the building.

Sunrise Worship Center

Reverend Sam Everett's church had just purchased a new campus and had held only a couple of services before Hurricane Michael came through Marianna. The facility only lost one awning. "The first Sunday we met under the breezeway and the following Sunday we had the electrical power back on," he shared. After that, his church became a distribution and feeding point giving out food, water, clothing and other supplies. They partnered with the American Red Cross, who was bringing three hot meals a day for about three months. "We fed people with all that American Red Cross left," Sam shared. They partnered with the Mormon Church, who were giving Sam's church supplies in bulk to distribute. They partnered with a church out of Destin and West Palm Beach, who were shipping supplies in by the truckloads. "We had staff working day and night distributing, and when we weren't distributing, we were unloading trucks trying to find a place to store it for distribution throughout the day," Sam shared. While it was hard work, he felt like it was well worth the effort.

Rivertown Community Church

Kevin Yoder spent the majority of Thursday trying to cut his way out with a chainsaw to the nearest County Road. When he arrived at the Marianna Church he assessed the damage with Senior Pastor, Paul Smith. Paul, seeing the need for a leader to step forward, asked Kevin to be the Point of Contact for recovery coordination. From that point forward Kevin coordinated relief efforts for the community. Kevin recalled, "as people showed up with requests, God met the needs right on time." Kevin never imagined how large a coordination effort he would lead, but God continued to bless his efforts every step of the way. Eventually, Kevin would assist in the creation of a long-term recovery group that will help the community for years to come.

CareerSource Chipola

Richard Williams lives in Bristol. "The day after the storm, I came up Highway 71 and drove into Marianna," he shared. "I grew up here, but couldn't find landmarks." He recalled being amazed when he saw the local bowling alley destroyed. He was even more shocked to find that there was only minor damage at the CareerSource Florida office.

Richard Williams remembered that for the first time ever, the United States Department of Labor released funds prior to the hurricane actually hitting land. "We were notified the funds were available in advance so when our management team gathered after the hurricane and we could move directly to recovery without having to worry about how to pay for the effort."

He arranged for management staff to come to work on Monday. The president of CareerSource Florida brought food and drinks to the office. "That was the best Coca-Cola I have ever had in my life," he shared. The office was tasked with getting disaster unemployment back up and rolling, so they could place people in jobs, especially to match up cleanup jobs. There was no Internet available. "We thought we were safe because of fiber-optics, but they were being cut with recovery." Richard continued, "crews came from Jacksonville and CareerSource North Florida with hotspots, extra cell phones, laptops and other supplies." The staff at CareerSource used the cell phones to help people.

When the rest of the staff returned, they were allowed to bring family. "I told them that we're going to take care of you, and if you need to leave, go," Richard shared. The staff responded well. "There was one employee that stayed in a trailer and in the last conversation the employee shared the siding was coming off," Richard explained. It would be three days later before they heard from this person. "I told the staff don't worry about a lunch hour, just go," he added. The staff was able to pick up hot plates of food from Eastside Baptist Church. "One lady on his staff had just come off of maternity leave, had damage to her home and at least seven people living with her, but she showed up daily all smiles," he shared. Richard bragged that there was no complaining in the office.

His staff took information out to the small towns, because gas was scarce. "Someone in Malone said to me 'just knowing someone from the outside came here means a lot to me,'" he shared.

Richard Williams making a plea to Florida Planners to assist at a Florida Chapter of the American Planning Association that took place at Florida State University's Doak Campbell Stadium Office Complex. Photo provided by Kay Dennis.

Kenny Griffin, Director of Business Services at CareerSource Chipola, shared that they were fortunate that their building was okay. The team was immediately able to process people who needed to apply for unemployment. "It was really more than applying for unemployment, because it brought them to a building that was stable and had air conditioning, and to a person that was willing to help," he shared. "We do not know yet why we had power." He was ready to move into the building just to soak up the air conditioning during those hot days following the storm.

Kenny shared a story about a man who showed up needing some gas. At first Kenny gave him directions to where he could find some fuel, but later learned the man did not have any money. Add to that, he had three kids with him. Kenny handed the man a twenty dollar bill and told him to go get some gas. Astonished the man replied "you don't even know me." Kenny said, "it doesn't matter." So, Kenny went out to patch his tire. The man jumped in and plugged Kenny's tire. Kenny said, "alright, we're even." Kenny's wife was running the distribution center in the Alford area, and he was working. So, he told the guy to go to his house and he would pay him to help with cleanup. The man showed up every day and worked for two weeks, while Kenny fed him, bought his gas and gave him money.

Kenny recalled how when Hurricane Michael hit his son's home, it did about $130 thousand in damage. His son tied the doors together to keep the air from coming through. Rain filled the house and they road it out. His son's wife had started cancer treatment two days prior to the storm. There were some people out of Alabama who showed up at their home after Hurricane Michael came through. They brought a travel trailer and a 50 gallon drum of gasoline, and gave it to them. Kenny shared his family didn't know who they were. Kenny's son, daughter-in-law and their two children lived in a storage building and that travel trailer for eight months, while she was going through cancer treatment. The couple was later able to rebuild and are now in their home.

Kenny's oldest son lives about a half mile away from him. They spent about five hours cutting trees so he could get out on the highway. Kenny and his neighbors started cutting in opposite directions to clear the roadway. After about a day the neighbors were able create a narrow path where vehicles could maneuver through to get supplies.

Kenny had about 80 acres of pines planted that Hurricane Michael destroyed. About 30 acres have been cleared. The remaining 50 acres is still on the ground. They loved living in a pine forest. While Kenny never depended on his pines for money, many people in the area were heavily involved in silviculture. It was their retirement, children's college fund, and livelihood. There is little left.

One of the problems that Kenny elaborated on with the livestock was with all the hay on the ground, it was just saturated with water. They were unable to plant winter grazing, because of the storm damage, making it difficult to get the cows through the winter.

Habitat for Humanity

Carmen immediately returned to work. "I felt that I had a place to go and others didn't," she shared. She had long days to start with traveling back and forth from Tallahassee until the weekend, but she enjoyed the reprieve from the storm damage. Carmen checked on her employees, and contacted every homeowner on their mortgage roll, doing damage assessments and helping them get in touch with the right people.

Carmen recalled that Hurricane Michael struck on pay week for the employees. She reached out to the Board of Directors, and explained how she was going to a Tallahassee branch of one of the banks they use and do separate withdrawals of each employee's pay in cash. Then, she would make them sign for it. She realized that issuing a check didn't make any sense with the banks down. Carmen hand delivered the cash to her employees at their homes.

While the Marianna Habitat for Humanity Office was slow to recover, the Chipley office recovered much faster. This enabled her to work out the Chipley location and have access to the Internet and contact who she needed. Habitat International sent down some volunteers to assist her team with providing aid to the homeowners, especially those with immediate needs. Others were reaching out with supplies for them, as well. Once the Marianna store was able to receive utilities, they used that space for supply distribution.

Carmen remembered how they had one employee who lived in Alford. He was completely trapped on his property. Staff from Habitat International and Big Bend Habitat were able to cut him out and try to secure, as best they could, his home. He would leave the area.

Carmen's home had to be reroofed, which didn't take place for eleven months. However, she pointed out that the waiting was due to the insurance and mortgage company. Carmen had only purchased the home months before the storm and hadn't built up equity in it. Carmen expressed that she knew she was knowledgeable and equipped to jump through the hoops, and it must have been worse for other people who may not have known how to navigate certain systems.

Carmen and her fiancé had planned their wedding date a year prior. After Hurricane Michael they didn't have as much time to dedicate to wedding planning. Carmen's focus was on construction of five quality homes each year. "After the storm I focused 100 percent on repairs, but that didn't last," she shared. Then, she was focused on serving more families and staying true to quality homes. "I wanted to make sure the families had homes they were proud of and where they could maintain their dignity, too."

Carmen married her fiancé on January 19, 2019 and the wedding was beautiful. The couple did not go on a honeymoon, because she was unable to plan one with everything going on. She was married on Saturday and back in the office on Tuesday. The only reason she wasn't back in the office on Monday was because it was a holiday. Carmen shared how she has penciled in a vacation three different times, but like many after the storm, it's hard to get away with so many responsibilities and the desire to help others.

Since the storm Carmen's grandmother lives with them full-time. Her grandmother's 1976 model single-wide mobile home survived the storm, but she had some fencing damage. Carmen and her fiancé' didn't have electricity for a very long time. "Often we see income disparities, but you know what?" she continued, "this hurricane put us on a level playing field in some ways". "Everyone, whether rich or poor, was affected and a sense of community came out of it," she shared. Carmen explained how she is concerned about people's ability to recover. Everyone does not have equitable access to resources. She went on to explain "in certain parts of town at night there was dead silence, but in neighborhoods like mine it wasn't silent because everyone had generators." There is still much work to be done in our community in addressing these types of issues.

Covenant Care

Jennifer Griffin, Hospice Care Navigator, shared that within a day the Covenant Care staff was out checking on their patients. They helped with placement, food resources, water and medication. The Covenant Care Corporate Office came in to support the local staff with hot meals, generators and pallets of supplies for many weeks. The executive leadership team with Covenant Care brought chain saws and helped cut paths to rescue those in need.

The Covenant Care Office was damaged, so the staff had to temporarily relocate to the conference room at the King Line Equipment, a tractor dealership just east of town. Also, Reverend Paul Smith allowed the team to use the back of Rivertown Community Church.

Jennifer's husband works for Century Link and had to report the day after the storm to restore services as quickly as possible. He was working 16 to 18 hour days working on destroyed infrastructure. Covenant worked with their employees during that time. Jennifer was allowed to bring her children to work with her.

Jackson County Association of Retarded Citizens (JCARC)

Jackson County Association of Retarded Citizens is a non-profit organization that provides day services and habilitation to developmentally disabled residents. The clients learn skills that enable them to live and work in the community. Hurricane Michael damaged the wood-shop and plant nursery to the point of closure. The organization's greenhouses were destroyed to the point of only having limited sales. One group home had to be evacuated. The residents moved away and nine employees were laid off. Another group home lost it's roof. According to Frances Henderson, Executive Director, electricity was out at one of the group homes for about 40 days.

Frances Henderson expressed her thankfulness for the people, who came in and helped from other ARCs in Florida, a Texas Baptist Men's Association, Mennonites from Atmore, Alabama and locals. Despite the blessings received, Frances found herself working with a smaller staff and less resources.

Partners for Pets

The only no-kill, not for profit organization in Jackson County, Partners for Pets experienced extreme damage on October 10th, 2018. The damage left Board of Directors Chair, Vicki Fuqua, questioning the future of the organization. Vicki's love for animals led her on a journey to fighting for a new facility in a new location. In the meanwhile, dogs are housed in 50 square foot kennels with Igloo brand houses that have been donated.

The Florida Caverns State Park

One of the natural treasures that Marianna is known for is the Florida Caverns State Park. The natural resources found within the park include caves and sensitive habitats for plants and animals. According to Billy Bailey, Assistant Park Manager, only about ten percent of the trees within the lush forests of the park remain and about half of the structures within the park were damaged. Interestingly, the original structures erected by the Civilian Conservation Corps and Works Progress Administration in the late 1930s survived with little damage. The park is hardly recognizable to locals.

Gift Shop Owner/Manager, Brenda Shiraz explained how on Friday, October 12th, she scaled a quarter mile of debris and large fallen trees to find missing water vessels and a rescue boat blown beneath a fence. A strike team was immediately activated by the Florida Department of Environmental Protection.

The very organizations communities seek help from were up and running, but at the same time suffering. Without outside help these organizations would not have been able to perform as well as they had. However, when facilities and homes are destroyed one wonders how long the people behind the services will remain in Marianna.

210

SURVIVING HURRICANE MICHAEL: A COMMUNITY'S STORY OF DEVASTATION, SURVIVAL AND HOPE DURING RECOVERY

While the community was working as hard as it could to help one another, more disasters would occur. One of the worst was that of fires.

Photos from Florida Caverns State Park provided by Brenda Shiraz.

PART IV

More Disasters

After Hurricane Michael came through Marianna there would be many disasters ahead. One common occurrence was wrecks from people passing through town trying to look at the damage rather than focusing on driving their automobile. Others would have wrecks related to running up quickly on a debris hauling truck or not being able to see well due to the large mounds of debris on the side of the road. There were fires daily for firefighters to respond.. Another common issue was accidental electrocution. There were several cases of people trying to clean up the fallen trees in the yard that resulted in the tree rolling onto them. One of our neighbors died from this type of accident. There were linemen who died because automobiles failed to follow traffic directions. Still others would fall and get injured from falls due to repairs. Another issue was the number of bees, and wasps outside, and lice found in the schools. All of these were particularly bad because the local hospital was transporting patients out and rescue workers were having a difficult time responding to emergency calls.

Chapter Nine

Fires

Fires were prevalent after Hurricane Michael. Rotting debris was fuel in the making for fires. Additionally, generators would be left on unattended and could possibly cause a fire when electricity returned to a home. Many homes had their roof lifted and wiring shook up from the storm leaving them vulnerable for such an event. This is one man's story.

Royce Reagan

"A few days after the storm I heard something pop downstairs and I smelled something." Royce Reagan explained. He investigated the sound and touched every outlet, turned every lamp on and off, and couldn't find a cause. At home they didn't have electricity, water, Internet or other luxuries, most have grown accustomed to enjoying. Thinking everything was fine, Royce's wife, Jackie, left for Bonifay to use a friend's Internet service in order to complete some assignments related to work. At the same time Royce made a trip to the lumber yard to work on his hurricane damaged home. An electrician had hooked up the generator and the couple felt comfortable leaving the generator running to preserve food in their freezer and refrigerator. Like most people with generators in the area, Royce and Jackie alternated the use of the generator with what was needed the most at the time. "We had been gone about thirty minutes max," Royce continued. "She was actually driving into Bonifay, when I called to tell her what was happening." A friend who drove by their house every morning before stopping at a convenience store for coffee, saw a little bit of smoke coming off the property and stopped about 7:30 a.m. to remind Royce that there was a burn ban. As the friend approached Royce's house he noticed smoke rising from under their home and called 911 for help. Their friend stepped out of the vehicle and took about four steps, when the front of the building exploded and the windows blew out. It seemed like the home had been fuming after the couple left. "He called me and said your house is on fire and I said quit kidding me, that's not funny" Royce continued. "Then, he said 'is anyone in your house?'" Royce added. "I knew with his tone of voice that it was serious, so I said no everyone is gone." His friend relayed that their home was on fire and it was bad. By the time Royce was able to return home, the fire was out. "There were 22 men in full-gear and three fire trucks, and Port Orange, Florida was the first one there," he continued.

There were several fire trucks staged across the street at Chipola College, because of the daily fires that were taking place after the storm. "They said an average of two fires a day," Royce conveyed. Clint confirmed how there were fires constantly. "A lot of that occurred as they were trying to get the grid back up," he shared. "As they powered up these houses, often there were shorts where the wind had blown and messed up the wiring," Clint continued. "Then shorts in the wiring would start fires." "Or you would have people who were trying to light fires to try to see and cook," Clint added about fires unexpectedly getting out of control. "We had generator fires," Clint continued. Another issue with the fires was due to the thunderstorms after Hurricane Michael, where dead trees were falling and continue to fall. "There was a house on the backside of the Cavern's that started catching on fire from where a limb hit a power line, and messed up that powering so that it arced and started a fire," Clint explained. With the trees down in the forest, and when it is dry, there is a high risk for fires. "There is so much debris and fuel on the ground, that it doesn't take much to start a fire." "The whole County was extremely lucky."

What it looked like when Royce drove to his house. Photo provided by Royce Reagan.

When Royce arrived, his family was waiting for him. He called Jackie, who turned around, without ever leaving her vehicle, to return to the remains of her home. Once Jackie arrived, she couldn't get to her home. She had to park down the street and walk in, because there were three more fire trucks and several fire-fighting units. Royce recalled meeting Jackie as she walked toward their home and saying "It is bad and there will be no divorce!" "So now when we get touchy, we just do like this," he made a gesture and smiled. "Get your butt off your shoulders, because there will be no divorce!" Despite the tremendous loss the couple hasn't sat down, cried and grieved as one might think. "We've cried a little, but not the real bad crying session," he added. Royce conveyed his physician told him he was probably in shock, but he refused to accept it. "I've had a few bad days, but I just say God has been good to me and I'm not going to complain about things," Royce shared.

Photo provided by Jackie Reagan.

Photo provided by Royce Reagan.

Ronnie Keel was cooking deer sausage for his neighbors and volunteers working the area when he learned his best friend, Royce, had a house fire. He thought the patrol officers weren't going to let him in at first, but he got there just as the fire had been put out. "I had been around there several times over those first few days following the storm, and he was proud that he didn't have a lot of house damage," Ronnie shared.

Royce gathered up the twenty-two firemen and took a photo. Royce shared, "I asked them, 'guys where do you want to eat lunch today?'" They met with 15 of the 22 firefighters at El Rio and bought them lunch. The other seven fire fighters were fighting a fire somewhere else. While they were eating Royce sang them a song about the Firemen's Ball that they laughed about. Royce later recorded the song and sent the song to the Firemen. The Fire Marshall was the first to respond and shot a video of the house on fire. "You could hear him in the video say 'guys put some water on the fire,' while they were still hooking it up," he continued. Royce shared that he could tell the Fire Marshall was the boss. After the fire was put out, the Fire Marshall prepared a report and showed Royce where he thought the fire had started.

Photo provided by
Royce Reagan.

The area was in the old part of Royce's house and the Fire Marshall believed that with the shaking of the house in the storm, one wire came loose. Royce described," they believe the wire was close to or touched another wire, which caused an arc that started the fire." "The Fire Marshall said 'Royce, if y'all had been asleep, it would have killed you,'" he continued. Royce and Jackie would not have had enough time to escape because when the fire blew, it was so hot that the entire house went up in flames.

Photo provided by Royce Reagan

Royce and Jackie had great insurance, but some things cannot be replaced. "I had a trumpet and a keyboard that went missing down there, and my video camera was sitting on the hearth next to the big screen where I was watching my grandson play ball," he recalled. While the camera was recognizable, it was burnt beyond any use. "I had scrapbooks with tabs on it for each grandchild" Royce recalled how he kept newspaper clippings, programs and other memorabilia. These books called "Super Grandchildren" were completely lost. "I couldn't find any remains" he sadly added. It was apparent how much he loved the scrapbooks. Royce also lost his grandmother's antique pump organ, which also held sentimental value.

The couple lost two computers, two tablets, and two phones. One phone was new. "Jackie was going to transfer her information over to the new phone, but they told her if you wait 22 days we'll do it for you and there won't be a charge" he continued. The can goods that did not burn, no longer had a label. However, according to Royce, most were fine. "We just opened up and if it tasted good, we ate" he shared. "If we didn't like it, we threw it away."

Left: Royce's Video Camera. Right: hearth in the Reagan home where Royce's video camera and "Super Grandchildren" scrapbooks were located at the time of the fire. Photo provided by Jackie Reagan.

Jackie and one of their grandchildren looking into the house after the fire. Photo provided by Royce Reagan.

The tin off the house Royce used to build a pole barn at their lake home. The couple is now living in a tiny house. Royce shared that Wilanne Daniels, the County Administrator, sent stacks of clothes for the great grandchild that is to be born in December. Wilanne also made Royce aware of valuable information about permitting that probably saved him time and money.

Other people were very generous to the Reagan family. "One lady in church gave my wife a one hundred dollar bill and said go buy you some underwear," he laughed sharing. "We had about twelve people who came up with cash money and said here," he continued. "The first one who gave it to us, I said we don't need the money, we'll make it!" "They said yes you do, you just don't realize it, because you can't replace everything you lost," Royce recalled. "A former student of mine gave us a thousand dollars," he shared. "Our mission's committee at church said why are we sending money to wherever when we have people in our own church and community who need it," Royce added about the money his church, First Baptist Church of Marianna, gave them. "First Baptist in Dothan, who I have served at twice in the last six years, sent our church five thousand dollars and said go find someone who needs it," he continued. The Director of Chipola Baptist Ministries told Royce to take photos of things that couldn't be repaired and he would present the photos before a meeting. A friend who formerly ran a western store, gave Royce clothes and lizard western boots from the store. Two or three men in town, who were about the same size as Royce, gave him some clothes. A local doctor's wife gave him some shoes that he recalled as "better than any shoes I've ever owned because they were perfect, and I love them!" At one point Royce and Jackie went to Chipola College, where they got some clothes, but felt like others needed them worse than they did. "We also had two groups come to our home and help use move trees," Royce shared.

Yet, Royce is not a person who sits around waiting for help. He helped others move trees, while others cut them. Royce shared how they knew the storm was coming but they didn't realize how bad it would be. The five or six storms that had come through the area previously, they had survived. "And this time we survived until our house caught on fire," he explained.

Natural and manmade disasters slowed down but did not stop recovery. While the community was trying to move past Hurricane Michael, recovery would be difficult. People remained in shock for months to come looking for ways to move past all that was lost while seeing the devastation daily.

PART V

Will Anything Be Normal Again?

Normal is often what we have grown accustomed to loving or being part of our everyday routine. In Marianna what the residents loved was lost. Yet, every day citizens had to look at the remains of the disaster as they drove to and from work. Representatives from FEMA shared with local government workers that they should keep the story alive and in the news, but at the same time, locals were finding it difficult to get away from the story. Every time they turned on their televisions or social media, the photos and stories haunted the ones living through the aftermath. The results can be emotionally traumatic and the recovery can seem very slow. Meanwhile, people continue to leave the area. Residents wonder how anything could ever be good again.

Chapter Nine

The Long Road to Emotional Recovery

While at work one day, someone asked me "do you, or anyone you know, have PTSD?" The question resulted in a pause. While I believed I certainly did not have it, I had noticed people freaking out about small rain showers coming through town. Then, when hurricane season started back up and I saw Hurricane Dorian headed in the general direction of Florida, I took note, as did others I knew. That's when I realized that emotional recovery is just as important as physical recovery. The daily haunting by our lost love was interfering and continues to interfere with our emotional recovery.

Mayor Williams

"You can just drive and see trees fallen," Mayor Williams explained. "It just reminds you of it." Mayor Williams expressed how he believed the psychological damage is going to remain for the rest of our lives. He believes many people have PTSD. "I think a lot of people got a profound respect for Mother Nature," he added. "When they tell me to leave, I think I will listen this time!"

Jim Dean, City Manager

After the initial responses were addressed, the City of Marianna transitioned to recovery. "It's still hard," Jim shared. "I worry about our staff being so tired, and about their mental health," he continued. According to Jim, "recovery is a slow and steady process of moving forward".

Marianna Public Works

"The good side of the storm was people let down their prejudices and learned to work together and become as one," Sam explained. "Our strength did not come in the number of people at that time, but from the unity of the people at that time." Sam expounded, "I feel like we've been on this emotional high and now we are coming back down to ground level" – reality. Yet, "there's still a sense of imbalance that causes an emotional rush," he continued. Sam clarified that Hurricane Michael was such a shock to the community that it will take some time for emotional recovery. "I saw the paranoia just with Dorian that was on the Atlantic side," he continued. "The people are still in panic mode and every little storm that they are hearing about they get in their mind that it is coming at us," Sam added. "We still have not landed on solid ground," or accepted the reality that is the new environment in Marianna. Sam projected that a couple of hurricane seasons out, the people may be more grounded. "There is still a lot of anxiety here, because when people heard about Dorian, they emptied all the water in Walmart," he continued. "You would think that it was in the Gulf!"

Marianna Fire Department

During the previous summer Clint had three deaths in the family. His paternal grandfather had passed away. His younger cousin had died following childbirth. Then, his maternal grandmother had died. Immediately following all the deaths, Hurricane Michael came through.

Clint explained that things are getting closer to normal at the Marianna Fire Department now. "We wound up getting on each other's nerves quite a bit," Clint shared. "Even before the storm, we lived together," he added. "We already got on each other's nerves a bit, but it was easier to deal with because we can hash it out," he added. "During the storm it got worse." "But one lady from a crew from down south told us 'it's bad and going to get worse, but once you come through this you'll be closer,'" he shared. "And sure enough, it did." The firefighters all had their moments, blowups, and ill words, but now they are closer. "We've always been close to be honest with you, but now we are closer because of what we've been through together," he added.

Clint explained that the fire fighters have post-traumatic stress. "I never had a lot of anxiety, depression or that type stuff before," he shared. "After the deaths in my family it really kinda hit me and I started having anxiety attacks," he continued. Clint shared an experience of where he was shopping in the Chipley Walmart one day and had symptoms similar to a heart attack. After taking a break outside he was okay, and realized it was anxiety. He explained that he never really understood anxiety and stress previously, because he never had experienced it. Clint clarified that he never liked bad weather. Yet, Clint added that he is not alone. "We all have it," he continued. On the flip side, Clint expressed feeling stronger and more confident in some ways for making it through Hurricane Michael and its aftermath.

"After a few days of living following the storm, people were getting pretty desperate," Brice Phillips shared. "We were trying to help, and they were going to sit there and cuss you," he elaborated. "After a while you just get tired and you're irritable and need some rest," he explained. Living in the aftermath of Hurricane Michael is emotionally draining. "I told my supervisor that if you don't keep people off of me, I'm fixin' to go monster jam here and start crushing cars." Brice was referring to the frustration of trying to clear the roads, while sightseers would be in the way. "You're trying to dig your way through to someone, and they are trying to go somewhere, and there is really no place for them to go." This is one type of stress that first responders felt when working after the storm.

Kim Applewhite

Kim shared that a few months after the storm, another smaller storm came through with wind, and she was a little scared. She remembered questioning whether or not they would be okay. Every storm since Hurricane Michael has dropped additional limbs and trees around all of us. However, now she's doing better.

Clay Wells

Clay Wells expressed that although he did not have any emotional problems resulting from the storm, he had learned a lesson. "I will not stick around for another storm!" The most trying part for Clay was balancing repairs at home and at work at the same time. Plus, Clay did not want to let the kids in the community down.

Corporal Mears

Mike described how he believes everyone here has a little PTSD. "I'm okay right now, but if a thunderstorm comes through, I get a little nervous," he clarified. "If the wind starts blowing, I start pacing the floors." While he feels like he can handle it, Mike experiences anxiety. Mike explained how he had noticed the same symptoms with others here.

Carmen Smith

In February she detected feelings of depression. Carmen remembers it took her a while to realize how depressed she was becoming. On top of the depression, she was exhausted and couldn't visualize an end in sight. She recalled how she was receiving more than thirty calls a day, and didn't have immediate answers as far as permanency and recovery. In addition, the volunteer base, which was the backbone of the organization, had their own personal destruction issues, and needed assistance. They weren't able to help the organization the same as in the past. "The support of the organization was struggling" she explained. Finding a balance with support and serving others was something constantly on the mind of Carmen. The self-controlled Carmen felt the weight and burden of Hurricane Michael's aftermath. "It took me a couple of months before I realized that this is not going to be quick and it's okay not to have those permanent and immediate answers," she continued. She decided to put a plan in place. Recognize that the plan is flexible and that it will take time. "I was having a conversation with my doctor, where we were griping to each other," she recalled. "She said 'Carmen we can't look left; we can't look right; we just have to look up!'"

Carmen expressed that she has seen people with PTSD. She remembered the possibility of Hurricane Dorian coming toward Florida and how people began immediately making preparations. There were hundreds of factors but one little line of probability on the spaghetti model just threw everyone into a panic in the area. Carmen shared that she always watched the news in order to plan for construction. However, now weekly, if not more often, she's on the National Hurricane Center's website. "I think it made our community more empathetic to the people in the Bahamas when Dorian hit them," she continued.

Father David Green

Father David explained how people in the area have gone through stages of recovery. "At first we were in shock and couldn't believe anything like this would happen in Marianna," he shared. "After that stage everyone pulled together and all the relief people were coming in," he continued. "During that period people were on kind of a high, because everyone is helping each other." People were meeting their neighbors and helping each other. "I had a neighbor who knocked on the door and asked what I needed, and the next morning I had it," Father David continued. "There was a certain amount of euphoria that was felt from helping one another."

Nothing lasts forever. "The relief people leave and you are left with massive debris everywhere," he added. The reality can lead to depression. "I used to walk in the neighborhood every morning, but it just got too depressing, because there were two houses that got trashed with trees and all the stuff was just on the street." Father David shared how living outside the City limits, some of the crews that came in to clean out the houses weren't required to dispose of the construction debris in a dumpster "We literally had toilets, TVs, insulation and junk on the street." It was so bad that he couldn't walk or drive in and out of the neighborhood without looking at mountains of junk

"Post-Traumatic Stress Syndrome is real," Father David clarified. "Even though I had been through all these hurricanes that actually had damaged properties we owned, in the past all I had to be concerned about was taking care of my family and my business." As a rector of a parish his concerns extended to his congregation. He reflected on all the other people within the parish with damaged homes or trailers or who had to leave and go live with relatives. "I got to the point where I wasn't sleeping well," he continued. Father David was overwhelmed by stress. "I think a lot of people have been through this trauma and it's good that I was able to talk to people about it." The Bishop made counselors available to Saint Luke's Episcopal Church for the minister and the entire congregation. "Episcopal Relief and Development sent a couple of men in from Colorado and Houston twice." He expressed how it was good to be able to talk to people who were familiar with disasters. "Not being able to worship in our church has made it more drawn out," he explained. "Such a beautiful house of worship and not being able to worship there adds to the anxiety."

Although worse than the other storms he went through, his personal situation was fine compared to other folks. Father David explained how just driving to the church each day and looking at the debris and ruins brings depression. "I can leave happy and be down by the time I drive six miles to the church." Recovery is a slow process and the town is still nowhere near back to normal. "It's rough."

Father David described how Hurricane Michael has affected the parish in multiple ways. "There have been funerals and weddings that we couldn't have there, because they would have been too large for the parish hall." "It's affected memorial services, burial services and weddings," he continued, "and that's a shame." However, Father David shared some of the positives of worshiping in the parish hall. "It's more casual, which provides for more interaction and a home-like feeling." "I've gotten quite use to it."

"I was able to leave and get away from it," he added. Father David addressed the importance of taking a break from your surroundings for a few days, so the stress doesn't drain your energy.

He went on to share about the generosity the church had received from his classmates from college to his seminary. "The parish that sent me to seminary raised $3K for our church."

He expressed how the children in the church were affected too. "Bad weather certainly has been stressful," he shared referring to the many raining days and small storms that brought down trees. "I've only been here four and half years – the people who have lived here all their lives must have more pain." Father David talked about how hot the summer of 2019 was with lack of shade. Prior to Hurricane Michael, Father David's neighborhood was buffered with beautiful trees. Without the buffer the neighborhood is exposed to highway traffic.

Immediately following the storm a man from Dothan showed up with a big generator, which enabled the church office to operate some equipment. He recalled how the church directory was outdated and on the computer. "We are better prepared now."

The good news for Saint Luke's Episcopal Church is the building can be repaired and insurance will pay. "There is absolutely no way I could handle all this without God." He continued, "I'm a control person and tend to want to do things my own way, but this was outside of my strength, control and capabilities and I realized that I had to have Jesus Christ and God's help." He added, "if anything, it has strengthened my faith." He shared how sometimes it's important to hit bottom, because then you realize how you need God's help. "I have certainly over the last year been through that."

Father David predicted recovery would take 10-15 years. He remembered Hurricane Katrina making landfall, and having one daughter in law school at Loyola, and another taking classes at Tulane. "The flooding was devastating. Recovery took about ten years."

"We had worst winds here," he recalled. "There is an amazing amount of trees gone." "It won't be the same and will take people a long time to get over it," he added.

Saint Luke's Episcopal Church over a year after Hurricane Michael. Photo provided by Kay Dennis.

Covenant Care

Jennifer Griffin described how bereavement is a journey. "It's never the same time, or the same way," she continued, "and people don't get cured, they just learn how to live with it." The people in Marianna needed a bereavement period following Hurricane Michael. Many had lost all of their belongings and the town they had grown to love during their lifetime.

Covenant Care recognized that not only were adults suffering, but so were the children. Many children were traumatized not only by what was lost, but by the experience they had endured. In response to the situation Covenant Care partnered with Play Big Therapy to provide "Camp Connect," a Saturday day camp available solely for children who had survived Hurricane Michael.

Chris Sikes

Chris Sikes believes the rise in deaths since Hurricane Michael may have been contributed to depression, not suicide. He noticed, mostly during services, that family members reported "they were never the same after Hurricane Michael."

Georgeann Adkison

Georgeann is still living with her uncle due to the number of fallen trees and the damage to her home. "My insurance company paid the claim on my home, but is about to drop my policy." So, now, Georgeann is trying to decide whether to rebuild or demolish her home. "Looking back, neighbors helped neighbors," which is exactly what Georgeann and Hancock Whitney Bank did. After the storm the bank donated $25,000 to the City of Marianna and to Panama City. Their Marianna branch has no issues. However, the Hwy 77 branch was demolished and they are operating out of a mobile trailer.

Joan Schairer

In January 2019 Joan's son purchased tickets to a show at the Fox Theater in Atlanta. Joan shared that it was the same weekend that tornadoes touched down and created damage on the east side of Alabama. When headed home on the Interstate 75, the winds picked up, small debris blew in the road and the rain began pouring at angle. Joan's son was driving, when she began screaming and reacting to the storm. After that incident, any time a storm came through the area, she had the same reaction. "When dear old Dorian appeared on the scene, my anxiety level was through the roof!" she explained. "My fear is I get moved in, and get all my stuff back, and then something else comes along," she shared. Joan later learned that her suffering was from all the stress in her life. Despite the stress, Joan added "I am very fortunate in the fact that I didn't lose my photo albums, and I didn't lose the personal things". Joan was also very grateful that her mother's sewing machine survived the storm.

Melissa Krebeck

Melissa laughed throughout her interview. Laughter can help get us through the tough times in life. While Melissa was sad about the natural environment and church, she wanted to replant trees. Melissa saw good in the family time shared after the storm. Melissa was sad about the church building, but felt the closeness of the members

"I remember the first storm after the hurricane, and I was a bit anxious," she shared. She went on to explain how her younger son, Evan, still struggles with some storm anxiety. While some of Melissa's anxiety has subsided, she admittedly focuses more attention on weather reports. Melissa's mother, Carolyn, also experienced some anxiety. Melissa shared "I had to promise my mom that I would never stay for another storm that would be a cat three or higher." Melissa went on to share how she had friends, who were trapped for about a day after the storm and were unable to return home until the beginning of August 2019. "Jason and Estelle Whiddon and some members of the Scout Troop got together with some chainsaws and helped them to get out of their house," she added.

Michelle Borden

Michelle's children did not walk away from Hurricane Michael without some emotional trauma. In November 2018, her son got kicked out of pre-kindergarten, because of behavioral issues. "I had nowhere to send him," Michelle explained. She got another daycare, but they would only let him stay one day. "Now I had to get him into a County school, because there aren't that many options in Marianna, and the ones that are available are full with hurricane displaced people," she continued. "Like I could afford to pay any more, I had to pay for a babysitter in December." She had taken a great deal of time off from work, so she could work with the County, and he could be enrolled in January. "He had two weeks of school in ,and then I left for Mississippi for two weeks," she added. They were able to get through the school year. She put her son in camp over the summer, and he was kicked out of camp. Michelle believes the upheaval with the storm triggered some of his problems. He would later be diagnosed with ADHD. Michelle's daughter thought Michelle was dead, when the trees fell on the bathroom in their home, and Michelle didn't come out quickly. "I never talk about the storm in front her, because she remembers that feeling that mommy is dead."

Shelby Durham

Shelby was pregnant and lost everything except what was most important during Hurricane Michael. Then, she had the physical stress from the heat and hard work of moving trees before she knew she was pregnant.

"I can remember how humbling it was to stand in a hot line waiting on food," she recalled. "I never dreamed I would be one of those people." "I never dreamed I would sit in a line for ice" she continued. "I never dreamed I would see NYPD in little Marianna, Florida." "That was surreal! Unbelievable!" Shelby shared how she still gets chills seeing the painted Xs on the houses. "I never dreamed that it would come in this far!" Shelby is thankful that she had a place to go.

238

Only one street away from where Matthew's parents lived, almost all the houses were destroyed. In fact, during the storm one of the neighbors called while running from room to room to seek safety from falling trees. Shelby shared that she is thankful that she is right where she needs to be with her mom. "I'm so thankful my mom is here!"

Shelby remembered feeling sorry for herself one day and saying "I'm displaced and I remember God saying 'you have not been displaced; you've been placed.'" "It still gives me goosebumps," she added. "At that point I was still in a little denial that life had changed so drastically in four hours."

Paula Livergood

Paula explained that she has a lot of PTSD. I have my ups and downs. I've had a lot of depression from it. "I have a lot of guilt, because I know my house is messed up, but it's not like some other peoples'." "It's been a struggle," she added. Paula hasn't received her money from her insurance company, SBA or FEMA. She only got an initial insurance check. She knows they owe her more, but there is guilt because other people are not getting the help they need. "It's just so hard when you get a contractor, they won't give you a quote, and you are constantly having to contact them," she explained. After a year, she still has water in the house, plumbing problems, air conditioning problems, foundation problems and much more. She shouldn't be living in her house, but the insurance company has not provided her another place to live while her home is being renovated and repaired. Paula is staying sick all the time from the mold in the air. "It's just hard because you are not prepared for that part of it," she continued. "You don't know what a hurricane is like until you live in it and you have to constantly deal with it," she added. "At this point, I will be happy if my house is fixed by next summer."

Paula and her kids live out of laundry baskets. Some of their belongings are in pods. Paula's father's home has mold in the insulation. "It's emotionally hard to see it," she explained. It was difficult for Paula when they had to remove her father's apartment and her childhood playhouse. While they knew the buildings would have to be demolished, seeing it was another level of anxiety for her family. "We watched while our memories were hauled away.

Paula finds it really hard to look at the pictures of the damage, but at the same time, she doesn't want to forget. "The hurricane has trickled down and affected so much of our way of life," Paula shared. Paula went on to explain how the terrain is so different now, and that everywhere you go you are reminded of the hurricane. "When I drive home, I dodge one pothole caused by the hurricane, and when I drive to work, I dodge another one," she shared. "When I pull in my driveway, I have to remind myself where to park, because some of the concrete was damaged from the trees falling." "I fall off my driveway a lot," she added.

"I try to picture the house looking better and the grass is already looking better," Paula shared about moving forward. Paul hopes to have the house and pool repaired within the next year. "I will always remember, but I want to get past some of the PTSD," she added.

Paula continues to cut trees down, because she and the children still hear the sound of the trees falling. "In June there was a storm that came through, trees fell and my cable line was knocked down over my driveway," she shared. Every time there is a storm, she questions which tree will fall this time. Just seeing the trees blowing brings back memories of sounds and experiences for Paula.

James Lash

James Lash described how when he drives through town "it hurts like you've lost something, like part of your family." "Even when I walk out in my yard and I've got no trees to walk under it

240

hurts," he continued. "Your whole life has changed." "This is something you don't hear about," James continued, "because the day after the storm comes, they quit talking about it." "The worst is yet to come after the thing leaves," he shared. "They are just getting the bank opened up right there across from the Post Office this week and it's been a year!" He went on to explain how the bank he uses is still not opened, but operating out of temporary travel trailer. "I tell you another thing that hurt, and I knew it was going to bother me, was when that first claw reached in and grabbed a hold of my home," he explained referring to when his house was demolished. "It near about tore my heart out." "He reached back in there and grabbed the refrigerator and throwed it on the pile," James sadly expressed. "It looked like he was throwing an apple." "And everything looks different," he continued. "It's hard to find what you are looking for, because it doesn't look like what you have always known."

Ronstance Pittman

Ronstance shared that when Dorian came she knew they were not waiting until the last minute. She watched it closely and was prepared to leave if necessary. Ronstance called this a new normal. She considered their family blessed, but added that their dog has a little PTSD.

Kisha Collins

Kisha Collins, a counselor with Life Management Center of Northwest Florida, evacuated to Birmingham before Hurricane Michael. When she returned, Kisha immediately went to work helping the community with emotional needs. She started at home with her family. Then, she continued her efforts by working in the local shelters where she could connect people to resources. At the shelters Kisha noticed how people were in shock, and often did not have their medications. She saw people who didn't have a home to return to or a change of clothes.

Five months after the storm, Kisha began interacting with North Florida Inland Long Term Recovery group as a Community Liaison for Life Management Center and Project H.O.P.E. Project H.O.P.E. is funded by FEMA, Florida Department of Children and Families (DCF), Substance Abuse and Mental Health Services Administration (SAMHSA), and Life Management Center of Northwest Florida. According to Kisha, the program started here after Hurricane Michael to provide "crisis counseling that would teach people how to discover their inner strengths, build resiliency and teach them to rely on their support systems." "Initially after the storm we went into heroism with neighbors taking care of neighbors," she explained. "By March the community was in the disillusionment stage, where they felt like everything should be back to normal," Kisha continued. "After the anniversary the community will go into a reconstruction and rebuilding phase." "This is when we will see people building bigger and better than before," Kisha added.

Mental health is important. The entire Community experienced some challenges and were forced to make adjustments following Hurricane Michael. Yet, it was nice to have free services available to teach people how to adapt to the new normal. A healthy community will be more successful at rebuilding better.

Chapter Ten
Town Recovery

Photo provided by Paula Livergood.

After Hurricane Michael stormed through town, Marianna was not only emotionally damaged, but also physically devastated. All the businesses were defaced, and some completely destroyed. People did not know if they had a job to which they could return. Housing was difficult to locate. People, whose homes had been destroyed, could not even find a hotel room within a hundred miles. It begs one to wonder how Marianna could ever recover?

Mayor Williams

"I think that one of the good things that came out of this was it forced you to get out of your comfort zone and mingle with people you would not normally mingle with and help people you wouldn't normally help," Mayor Williams shared. There were people without a house helping other people, who didn't have a house. "I think the Lord was able to shine through the situation."

"Now the shelter was something, with everyone at the high school; it was a mess!" Mayor Williams, a math teacher at Marianna High School, saw first-hand the state of the shelter. School officials were constantly monitoring the building, which had animals in it. It was important to get the children back to school as quickly as possible, because they needed some normalcy and their parents needed to work. The kids couldn't return to school until the shelter was empty and it had been cleaned up.

"We are still hauling off debris and will be doing that for a while!" he continued. Commissioner Williams became Mayor eight month after Hurricane Michael, which he believed to be the most difficult time. "The worst thing was becoming mayor in the middle, because our revenue had and is still decreasing drastically," he shared. "You have to tell people who have been dedicated to helping us get over this!" "You can't give them a raise," he added. "We are losing thousands and thousands of dollars every single month as a result of the storm, which is really causing a deficit," he continued. Mayor Williams went on to explain that he was concerned about the upcoming census due to the number of people who have been displaced. "If the census numbers go down the City of Marianna's access to Federal money will be affected for ten years," Mayor Williams clarified. He went on to share how the City of Marianna's income is already reduced. "The Federal Prison alone is about $20 thousand a month in lost revenue, plus the headcount at the prison is lost," he added. "That is just utilities revenue, that doesn't include jobs and when people go to other cities and spend their money in other places," he shared. Mayor Williams expressed his concern about the City's housing crisis. "I know the type of housing is going to be crucial!"

As far as economic development goes, "I think everyone is working hard to try to create things," he continued. "As of right now, we have so many other priorities," Mayor Williams added. "First, we have to build houses for people to live in, so we can accommodate people working in those businesses," Mayor Williams explained. He remembered Outback Steakhouse and Chick-fil-A bringing in food for the community. "It is important that we not forget to patronize our businesses."

Mayor Williams spoke about spending more money than he intended to spend cleaning up the community. He recalled price gouging. "You get to the point where you have to get something done," he shared. "It's depressing to walk out of your house and not even see your yard." "There was a church group, and I don't know where they were from," Mayor Williams continued. "We were out helping another guy in the community and they just started sawing and moving limbs for nothing." "When we saw people helping, we would go and feed them," he added. "I had a lot of breakfast sandwiches in my freezer, and since I had a generator, I would heat them up and walk through the neighborhood and passing out sausage biscuits I had warmed up in the microwave." Mayor Williams continued "I couldn't sleep, so I might as well do something good." "They were selling bottled water at one store for $20 a pack that was normally sold for $2.99," he recalled. "Yet, when you run out of water, you would pay $20 for that water," he added.

"We did a good thing by getting our gas up and running, because we were the ones suffering, but I think Dothan made millions of dollars daily off our residents, just off of generators, gas and food," he shared. Mayor Williams remembered spending well over a thousand dollars at Lowe's purchasing a generator for his family and his parents. "That was just one day and there was a ton of people behind me buying them just that one day," he added. There are some generators that you can run your whole house on, but most people had the type where you had to pick and choose what appliances and how much electricity to run. "I bought a window unit because I just couldn't take it anymore."

246

Like many families, they lived mostly in that one room with the air conditioning, because of the extreme heat.

"The saddest thing was seeing Old Saint Luke," Mayor Williams shared. "That is where I went to church when I was little."

Saint Luke Baptist Church. Photo provided by Rhonda Dykes.

"I really don't think we will ever fully recover," Mayor Williams explained. "I think the damage is done." Yet, he plans to rebuild better than ever. "I want to make sure the things we are replacing with are better than what was there before." Mayor Williams shared how he thinks it is important that we see it through, while keeping the morale of the people up. "Like making sure our fireworks are special every year," he elaborated. "We can remember, but focus on the positive things, the relationships that were built, the trust that was formed, and the faith that was strengthened."

"I'm really worried about the health issue because we lost a lot of trees and that's where we get our oxygen from," he explained. "We don't really know about the long-term effects of all these trees missing," he continued. "This is always been a place with the rivers, and you know, you just want to be outside," he explained. I knew, understood and longed for the natural beauty he described.

Police Chief Hayes Baggett

Becky Partin sadly explained "it's going to take years to recover, I imagine." Lieutenant Stroud added, "we were overshadowed by Bay County, who had immediate resources." Chief Baggett clarified, "it's because Hurricane Michael did not hit a population center that we did not receive needed national attention." "What we had was a pristine natural environment impacted," Hayes continued. "The surviving trees were twisted and beetles became a problem." Lieutenant Stroud commented on how rebuilding resources were diverted to Bay County, and how the area was overshadowed by the election. "Because of the election that immediately followed Hurricane Michael and the California fires, we had to fight for assistance," Chief Baggett explained. "We are going to try to be more prepared." This was a sentiment repeated daily to me by many.

Marianna Fire Department

Clint shared that he felt like the City of Marianna is doing the best they can probably do. "I'm concerned with the population, and business," he explained. "The storm brought in some people and it also took out some people." "We have a very big exchange of people that we know and are used to, and people we don't know and we're not used to," he continued. Clint talked about the heavier traffic since the storm. "There are people here, and I don't know where they are coming from or where they are going." Unfortunately, not everyone that came into the community was good. Now without the trees blocking the wind, Clint shared that he believes the town is more exposed to the elements should another storm come this way. Plus trees continue to fall with smallest amount of rain.

Kim Applewhite, City Clerk/Finance Director

"What I noticed personally is that Michael didn't get the publicity, and I see this on social media and the news, but it is really true when you look back and see the devastation," Kim Applewhite explained. "I mean, basically Mexico Beach was annihilated and we didn't get the focus and the financial contributions that other places even with a category three got," she added. Kim shared how she noticed it from the beginning and still doesn't understand why. She clarified that local government money is all provided upfront. "I've read some articles, and it seems like other category three hurricanes got a lot more personal contributions, not counting government money, that we didn't get," Kim added referring to fundraisers, benefits and events where big singers and famous people were brought in to assist. "That was a little disappointing."

Kim expounded on how our community and others have a long way to go. She shared how she pulled over for gas a year after the storm in Port St. Joe and found the gas station open, but working out of a tent taking cash for fuel purchases. "In Mexico Beach a year later there is still no gas station or grocery store open!" "That's almost unreal," Kim continued. "I know it takes time, but even in our town you still see blue tarps everywhere, people who haven't fixed roofs, and devastation everywhere," she added. Many people are still waiting for contractors and insurance adjusters.

"Personally, I've had terrible dealings with insurance adjusters," Kim shared. "I had to hire a public adjuster, because they wouldn't fix my house," she continued. "A year after a major category five hurricane you shouldn't have to beg your insurance company to fix your home!"

Kim explained that she has a cousin, who lives in Mexico Beach several blocks off the water. While her cousin's home endured lots of damage, it was standing, but everything around it is gone. "Mexico Beach is just the most depressing thing I've ever seen," Kim shared. "When you see all the devastation, you have to wonder why this area didn't get the attention."

A year later Kim and her staff are trying to figure out how to recover as a City. "We lost one of our major customers, the Federal Prison, and Ice River Springs," Kim explained as a major City utility revenue loss. "How do we move forward with our budget and recover until we can get our customers up and running?" "Between the Federal Prison, Ice River Springs and about 120 homes that have not reconnected to City utilities, we are probably talking a loss of about a million dollars in revenue in a year," she clarified. "By the time the Federal Prison gets up and running, and we recover the 120 homes, we will have lost millions of dollars in revenue."

The City had upfront costs related to cleanup. There has been some insurance reimbursement that has helped. "FEMA takes a while and that is just the nature of it, and we haven't had much come in yet," she explained. "It's usually a year or two process before you get your money back from FEMA," she added "and you have to continue to pay these vendors who are fixing stuff." "The Catalyst Building repairs was a three million dollar project, but they employee a lot of people," she continued. "There was three to five million dollars in losses in just that one building, not counting all our other losses," Kim added. "We will definitely be in the tens of millions of dollars in losses before we get through, but hopefully our insurance and FEMA will help us!" "So, we just have to figure out how to rearrange things for a while," she continued. "I think we are going to be fine eventually, but it's just going to take time, and it just shows you what financial uncertainty we are dealing with," she added. "It could be two or three years before we figure out our total loss."

The Clerk's Office was very busy upfront, but continues to be super busy. "We are just trying to make it through another year, but it's just crazy busy!" At first Kim and her staff had to get back up and running without delays, and she went on to explain that "now we are dealing with FEMA, which is a huge deal financial-wise because of the reporting required for audits." Kim predicts for the next three to five years they will be dealing with massive amounts of paperwork for FEMA, insurance and extra grants, if the City is fortunate. "Audit requirements are just going to go through the roof," Kim shared. "I spoke to the auditor last week and she explained that there will be massive amounts of time added to the audit for this paperwork, which will cost the City more money," Kim continued. "That's going to go on for years."

"We will never be okay, but from a City perspective we will be fine, it's just going to take a little time," Kim added. "Without reserves we would be out borrowing money, doing bond issues, having the cost of doing bond issues, and trying to find the money to pay for the costs," she clarified "We are about to start private property debris removal, which could cost us around $3 million upfront," Kim explained. Reimbursement will take time. "We are starting to feel some of the effects of what's next."

One thing Kim didn't share is that having more work, doesn't mean the City will hire more people. Like the Clerk's Office, every City department is busy with many times more their normal workload and the same number of people.

A year later Kim is still in litigation with her insurance company regarding the damage of her home. "I have mold around my windows that keeps growing thicker every day," she stated with exasperation. She didn't have any trees on her house, but the windows were compromised by the storm. Some of the windows are broken and every time it rains, she notices the moisture coming in. All of her windows have to be replaced, in addition to, mold remediation. "Here we are one year after and we are just getting to the point of coming up with the estimates for the damage," she added. With contractors being booked out for years, Kim projects at least another year before her house is in a livable condition. "What disappoints me is nobody that goes through a category five hurricane should have to be treated like that!" "I think it's inexcusable," Kim added.

Kim's mother's home had about $50 thousand in damage, but her mother's insurance company was good to help. Kim's daughter and brother were also able to get needed repairs with the help of the insurance companies, but her sister still has a tarp on her roof, because she didn't have any insurance. "There are still people who are suffering, because they didn't have insurance and the resources to put a $30 thousand roof on their home," Kim added. Those people are not only dealing with how to get a loan, but also how to pay for materials and contractor prices, which are inflated following the storm.

Clay Wells, Parks and Recreation Director

Clay Wells shared that the rebuilding of the Recreational Department and facilities began about two weeks after Hurricane Michael. "Nothing is fast!" Clay explained how his staff had to create an inventory of damages on the eleven parks he manages. After the storm Jennings Field was used for a debris field. The pavilion there collapsed during the storm. That park will have to be completely rebuilt. "We are just waiting on the insurance company to say what they are going to give us and the City Commission to say how to move forward," he continued.

It was mid-January before Clay and his team were able to go back into their office complex. During those first couple of months, they operated out of a 400 square foot concession stand across the street. "We cancelled the remainder of soccer season in 2018 and football season, because it was not playable," Clay explained. "We knew come January that we at least needed to get our basketball program up and running," he shared. Clay was able to do that at the local public schools. "We had to really bust our butts to get our fields ready for baseball and softball, our biggest season," he continued. Clay was able to get everything that was necessary repaired before the season. The fences and some other things were temporarily repaired so the area youth could play baseball and softball. One year later the M.E.R.E. is 100% complete. "Which I feel proud that we were able to get everything done in less than a year," Clay shared. Clay and his staff had to ensure all park lights were reinstalled and straightened, which cost about $70 thousand. He shared how they spent about $30 thousand in fence work, and that's not counting building repairs. "The biggest insurance problem we had was that everything out there and around town has different deductibles, even a four foot fence to a six foot fence, if you can imagine that," he continued. "Lights on the fields had different deductibles, so you had to figure field by field," he added. "Everything had to be figured individually, like scoreboards, batting cages, and that was the biggest issue." Clay had to figure long lists of line items for each City park and recreational field.

"Wynn Street Park has trees down everywhere," Clay explained. "One of the debris haulers who was staying at the M.E.R.E. RV Park told me 'Man, I've seen more structural damage, but I've never seen more damage the way you guys have got it from here to the coast,'" Clay shared. Wynn Street Park did have some swings and fence damage, but primarily fallen trees and debris cleanup. The cleanup has been slow with some of the other parks, as well. Their primary concentration was at the M.E.R.E. Complex because that was where the youth activities were located. All the other City parks are completely functional, other than Jennings Field, and a portion of that is functional now.

At home, Clay was able to make all necessary repairs with his insurance, with the exception of the fence, which is still being repaired. "What I have found with me and most of my friends, we worked like hell for a few months," he explained. "Then, we kinda got tired of it all and put it down for a while." "My plan is, when it cools off this winter, to finish everything up."

Jimmy Grant

Almost a year later, permits have only eased up a little, but Jimmy Grant now has time to work on his yard. "There are probably at least 50 out-of-area new contractors, and we need even more," he explained. "Most are booked out for months ahead," Jimmy added. While there are many good stories about people helping people, one sad issue Jimmy has seen is contractors that have financially hurt people in the area. "It only takes a few to make it really bad," Jimmy shared. "Unscrupulous and mostly unlicensed contractors have misled folks in Marianna." The road to recovery is long with permitting. Jimmy estimates three or more years before the roofs on all buildings with tarps are repaired. "Some will never be repaired," he stated sadly.

Wilanne Daniels

In November Wilanne was selected by the Jackson County Board of County Commissioners to be the County Administrator. According to Wilanne, there were many County government buildings and parks damaged. "We are estimating about $32 million dollars to public property owned by Jackson County," she shared. "With the debris haulers and everything, we are estimating approximately $70 million in damage to roads," Wilanne added. In November, Jackson County advertised for Disaster Recovery specialists and hired GP Strategies to handle public assistance. More recently Jackson County began working on a Disaster Recovery Plan. "The actual repairing of all the buildings will be a very slow process, because you take it one step at a time," Wilanne explained. "We have no additional staff than we had before the storm, so we are still doing our regular jobs plus recovery," she added.

"In January GP Strategies was able to take off," Wilanne shared. Over the next several months, the focus was on public assistance and debris. Simultaneously, Wilanne was working with the North Florida Inland Long-term Recovery Group and becoming very involved in the local government committee as chairman. This meant staying in contact with committee members on various things and trying to identify needs in the community that the local government would be appropriate to address. If not a local governmental issue, then she would pass the need on to another committee, who could better address the issue.

"During this time there were things I learned," Wilanne shared referring to how she wasn't provided a handbook. "When a community is going through this type of disaster, people need some normalcy as quickly as possible," she added. Wilanne probably had many topics on her mind, but chose to focus on Blue Springs. Blue Springs has been historically popular to the area. "We almost made a monumental error with the thought processes behind not opening Blue Springs," Wilanne continued. "We were already scheduled for some work to be done with the head wall, and the thought was, while it is completely in disarray, we could go ahead and get that work started." Wilanne clarified that the park was scheduled to open the following year and the cleanup would look really nice. For that reason Chipola College was not notified that a lifeguard class was needed. "When we received a ton of backlash, I realized what that meant to the community," Wilanne continued. She explained how when she provided information about debris pickup, apeople may or may not comment on social media. However, Wilanne recalled that one post she made about Blue Springs received more than 25,000 views. "I realized it wasn't that every single person would go to Blue Springs, but that was another blow to the community all these months later," she added. Once Wilanne realized that she had underestimated the power of what encouragement it would be to the community to see Blue Springs open, she and her staff quickly made things happen. "Rhett Daniels did a beautiful job pulling that off," she continued. "I personally had to take that responsibility by not being more proactive with Blue Springs, and I learned a huge lesson in that the community needed that to be returned to normal," Wilanne added. She clarified that it was a great season at Blue Springs, but the numbers were much lower than normal. "It has been really, really amazing to see how everyone in the community has played their part."

Blue Springs after Hurricane Michael. Photos provided by Rhonda Dykes.

Corporal Mears

"In essence, after the storm hit, for lack of a better term, we were knocked back into the Stone Age," Mike explained. "It put everyone in this County on the same playing field." "We all came together in this County and helped each other," he continued. "This County is exhausted in the cleanup alone," Mike shared. "I saw it first-hand, how government had to pay for cleanup up-front and wait," he added. Mike shared how many of the local churches donated food, shelter and supplies. Local businesses helped too, especially when he was at his most desperate moment.

Mike believes the area is recovering well, but it will be a minimum of five years before we have any normalcy. "It's going to take that long just to finish cleaning up," Mike shared. "As far as the beautiful trees and canopied streets we had here, and that is something I always took for granted, it's gone; we probably won't see that in our lifetime." Mike shared he believed full recovery would take ten years. Mike loved being outdoors and was clearly saddened about the state of the natural environment.

Kevin Daniel

Kevin Daniel explained that Jackson Hospital has a State grant to install a potable water system, a new well and water tank, so they will be better prepared in the future.

Tiffany Garling

Tiffany shared how it's easy to get back into a routine and forget. Yet, on July 22nd, over nine months after Hurricane Michael, Florida Public Utilities informed the Chamber that "30 percent or over 500 houses were still not back online in Jackson County." Many were destroyed and people were not returning. Hurricane Michael costs for Florida Public Utilities exceeded $70 million. Tiffany believes that economic development is important now. "We have got to have a factory or high energy consumer to make up the loss for the power company."

Stuart Wiggins

Stuart Wiggins, Director of Facilities for Jackson County School Board, explained that Jackson County had hurricane damages in excess of $11 million. Approximately $320 thousand was in school fencing. One million dollars was spent on repairs to school facilities throughout the Jackson County. Not only were buildings in need of repairs, but also scoreboards, bleachers, signs, and field lighting.

Marianna Middle School after Hurricane Michael. Left: Photo provided by Rhonda Dykes. Right: Photo provided by Scott Hagan.

Despite the millions of dollars in damage, Stuart is moving forward with future improvements for Jackson County Schools, including the $60 million K-8 school scheduled to open in August 2020. Stuart shared that combining schools will save taxpayers $300 thousand annually.

Kenny Griffin

Kenny Griffin clarified very eloquently "a piece of paper with some numbers on it, don't mean a thing if you don't focus on the people." Similarly, focusing on programs may not be successful with people. In other words, an agency can't have a successful program that fails people. "We should always put people first and make sure our best efforts are towards a person, because they are the reason for the program," he added. Kenny expounded that recovery is a long process, and that we will be long since retired before it's over. "Recovery, of course, will take many years, and when we have completed it, we won't even know we've completed it," he continued. "And when it is completed, there will be a younger generation who won't remember what it was like before the storm."

Carmen Smith

Carmen shared how her Habitat for Humanity homeowners had their mortgage insurance escrowed in, which probably means they are not the best at keeping up with their homeowner's insurance. Fortunately, they had Carmen a professional at knowing how to handle insurance issues. She described how she would hear people complaining about their dealings with their insurance companies. "I get it but I've had to deal with 20 to 30 people's insurance claims."

Carmen clarified that moving forward and looking at the continuum or "pathways to permanency," she is trying to shorten the time people are exposed to vulnerabilities. For this reason Carmen and her team at Habitat for Humanity are actively seeking funding to not only build new houses, but make existing structures livable, as quickly as possible. She continued to share that even when focusing and working on a demolition and rebuild, she is trying to limit the time people are displaced.

Carmen is aware that what may be considered affordable in other areas, is not affordable for people in Marianna. She is constantly looking for ways to cut costs and help citizens with lower mortgage payments. They build to fortified standards and energy efficiency without having the certifications, because certifications cost money. "Now we are seeing the importance of certifications in that having the homes certified will open doors for additional funding for the organization," she added.

Carmen received a call from Tiffany Garling, who put her in contact with Kevin Yoder about being involved with the recovery group. "In hindsight Rodney Andreasen, the Jackson County Emergency Management Director, told us we needed a recovery organization, and we had tried to get that off the ground," she continued. "The name of the organization was 'Together Everyone Achieves Recovery.'" Carmen explained how the Red Cross, Jackson County Emergency Management, Jackson County E911, County Fire Chief, City of Marianna Fire Chief attended the meetings to be ready for a disaster. It never really gained the momentum needed, because of lack of community support. According to Carmen the last meeting of that team was in June 2017, because no one really believed a disaster like Hurricane Michael would take place in Jackson County. Tiffany knew she had been involved before and Carmen came to the table immediately and began assisting. Carmen is the secretary and on the Board of Directors.

Jackson County has lost a great deal of housing, but it was needed before the storm. "We have an opportunity to look at the different types of housing and 'not be cookie-cutter in our approach,'" she clarified. Carmen wants to incorporate the aspect of dignity for her homeowners. "The beauty of our service is where the construction aspect is black and white, the social service aspect is not," she continued. While Habitat for Humanity has a retail aspect where profit is important, they will donate in social service situations. It is important to Carmen that families can make a purchase from their Restore without having a stigma attached. While she believes it will never be what it once was, Carmen is hoping the community will be better.

Guardian Ad Litem

Jane Powell, Guardian Ad Litem Advocate Manager, explained "we lost volunteers that lost their homes that ended up moving away, or they were so devastated that we had to take their cases back, because they didn't have enough time to handle everything." "We were also personally affected," she added. Best Interest Attorney Eric Love expressed, "case management lost a significant number of their case workers." These volunteer and case worker losses make it difficult for the organization to fight for the children in the community.

Father David Green

Saint Luke's Episcopal Church has still not been restored. The more the mitigation team worked on the structure, the more problems they found. The structural engineers came out in April to evaluate the building, but their report was not provided to the parish until August. Little was done during that time because of the need to read the engineer's report. There was a meeting between the Church's insurance company and the construction company. While the parish thought they were waiting on the two groups to come up with a plan, it turned out that the parish was responsible for it. The miscommunication cost more time. The parish hired a local architect to evaluate how to make the structure sound while maintaining its historic character. "I thought we were getting somewhere when they finally took the old roof off," Father David shared. "It's a historic building and everything has been delayed because of that, and due to a small amount of asbestos in the shingles." "As it turned out they took the roof off way too early," Father David continued. They couldn't put a new roof on the structure until the engineer's report was complete. "So, they covered the roof with tarps that have torn and had to be replaced multiple times," he added. "We kinda took a step back instead of forward."

The structural engineer's report explained the leaves Father David had seen in the church on his initial visit after the storm. "It's a term called racking," Father David clarified. "There was enough wind and pressure that got inside the church building that it actually lifted the roof," he continued. Looking at the building you wouldn't be able to notice. Some of the structural beams were damaged. It was determined at some point during the storm the exterior brick wall that faces Lafayette Street was separated from the interior brick wall on the same side near the roof line about three inches. An extensive amount of work is expected to return the church to the pre-storm state.

Partners for Pets

Vicki Fuqua and the Board of Directors for Partners for Pets are still in negotiations with the Jackson County Board of County Commissioners regarding the future of Partners for Pets. In times when local governments are cutting funding to focus on repairs and recovery, it has been difficult for the group to receive the funding they need. However, there have been several groups, who have helped raise money for the organization. In October 2019 the organization had a fund raiser called "Petoberfest." The tenacious Vicki Fuqua loves pets and will continue to fight for this worthy cause.

Florida Caverns State Park

Eight months after Hurricane Michael, in excess of 100 State employees arrived at the Florida Caverns State Park on June 14th to participate in "A One DEP Work Day." There was more than 16 inches of rain that came into the cave during Hurricane Michael due to tree roots at the original cave entrance. After the storm more than three inches every week over a period of time had accumulated inside. The result was debris and mud preventing park operations. Six hundred feet of corridors were cleared by the volunteers.

On the first day of July the park opened with limited access, due to the need to clear trails by hand to preserve natural resources and the caves. The park held a ribbon cutting on July 10th. By mid-July the Hickory Pavilion had opened. The park continues to work towards a goal of being fully operational on Earth Day in 2020.

Spears Café

The weekend before Thanksgiving, Coe Spears, owner of Spears Café was helping his family with some home repairs, when he fell from a ladder and broke his leg in two places. The injury required surgery, two screws and a rod. Despite their quaint café surviving the storm, they had to close the business temporarily, so he could recover. As Coe was better able to get around, the café was re-opened during limited hours. Spears Café is now better than ever.

Keith Armondi

Local contractor and business owner Keith Armondi, owner of Armondi Roofing, provided a little insight into the world of contractors following a natural disaster. "After Hurricane Michael, a lot of local contractors went to Panama City because they were able to earn more money." Keith explained how with fewer contractors available there was some price gouging taking place. Rather than leave for money, Keith decided to stay loyal and help his customers. "At first the storm brought out the good in people, but it also brought out the grouchy side due to lack of patience in customers waiting for work to be done," he added. "I'm booked out until July 2020, and still receiving requests daily." "Another problem after the storm was people going around charging residents $50 for an estimate on repairs," he continued. "No one here does that!" Local contractors provide free estimates. Finally, Keith shared how some contractors are not certified and are taking advantage of people while they are down. Keith recalled one of the major differences between Hurricane Andrew and Hurricane Michael was the number of trees. "After Hurricane Andrew, you could see for miles, while here there were trees everywhere", he shared.

Jordan Miles, CNM

After Hurricane Michael came through Marianna, there was a baby boom in the area. Add to this dilemma that one of the labor and delivery options in Panama City was unavailable. This situation brought Jackson County native Jordan Miles back home to work at Chipola Surgical and Medical Specialties, OB/GYN to help expecting mothers.

Jay James

Jay's business partner, Jack Brown, had an apartment that came available. However, she remembered it was nasty because of the previous tenants. Her partner paid for new carpet, linoleum and paint. Yet, the handyman didn't show up to do the work. When he finally showed up drunk, they hired another man.

The family was able to move in one week before Thanksgiving, and Jay's mother-in-law was able to move back home. Jay shared that they never ate a meal there, because of what they had seen. They had a washing machine and dryer. The insurance company paid for rentable furniture, electronics, dish towels and other needed supplies at a cost of $1000 a month. Their rent was $400 a month.

While staying in the apartment they had to obtain a restraining order on a person dressed in black claiming to be stalked by the President of the United States. The same individual danced before them and started fires. Finally, this woman was arrested for terrorizing the neighbors.

In February, Jay's insurance company totaled her home and mobile home. While they didn't receive as much for the contents as they had hoped, they were pleased to be able to rebuild. Since their costs were so high renting and she was concerned they would run out of money too soon, Jay asked the rental company to pick up all but two beds. Then, the family went to America's Home Place and designed their dream home.

Later that same month Jay's partner, Jack Brown, passed away. She explained how she had been heartbroken. The partners had shared a close bond and he had been a mentor to Jay. Jay shared how she missed his jokes.

In April, Jay purchased new beds, mattresses and plastic stands for their clothes. While her new home was being built, the family wrote their favorite Bible scriptures on the home's beams. They also saved a few bricks that were her childhood home's bricks to be used in the new home. In late October of 2019, over a year later, Jay and her family would move into their new home.

Joan Schairer

"Towards the end of October my mother had to either leave rehab or go into the nursing home, and because we had nothing, I couldn't take care of her anyway," Joan explained. Marianna Health and Rehab had generators and was close to Jackson hospital, which relieved Joan from unnecessary worry. Joan shared that she was "well-pleased" with Marianna Health and Rehab.

Joan continued to live in her home until the electricity was reconnected around November 1st at her mother's home. "Florida Public Utilities came out and pulled my meter," Joan shared. Operation of generators is expensive and often, limited. A year later Joan is still living at her mother's home. Meanwhile, she worked with her mother's insurance company to ensure everything was repaired. Repairs required getting on a waiting list with a contractor. On Thanksgiving Day Joan's mother's roof was repaired. The garage was repaired near the end of December and the window was repaired in January.

Joan continued to call daily regarding the blue tarps not keeping the inside of her home dry. In January, after three months of rain pouring, the insurance adjuster instructed Joan to have a temporary power pole installed so contractors could have electrical power for their construction equipment. This also enabled Joan to remove water that was about ankle deep in her home.

"Through all of this my mother's health continues to decline" Joan recalled. "She had been diagnosed with dementia and never walked again." Despite Lois's attempts to walk, she had not been able to progress when her rehab time ran out towards the end of October. Swallowing had become a problem for her, as well. Lois's 97th birthday was on February 27th and about 1:30 a.m. on the 28th, Lois died. The funeral was delayed until March 8th to allow time for family to arrive. On March 7th, Joan received a call from the foreman, who was ready to go to work. Very pleased, Joan went to her home to retrieve some items. "He said 'Joan, why didn't you tell me your mom had passed away?'" Joan recalled. "We could do this later." Joan replied "no, no, no, mom understands." The day of Lois's funeral, the contractors began working.

After they reroofed the house in mid-March, the waiting game began because contractors were booked out for years. Then, the storm the mitigation team visited Joan's home and a misunderstanding occurred over saving the kitchen cabinets, because the man was deaf. "I rounded the corner just in time to see him pick-up a sledge hammer and almost destroy my cabinets," she explained. The mitigation team failed to bring a pod or boxes, which were promised. "My stuff got thrown all over the living room, clothes included," she said with exasperation. Joan was finally able to store her belongings in the old Roller Rink building just west of town on May 21st, more than seven months after Hurricane Michael.

On September 23rd the garage door was installed. Joan is still waiting on the flooring and the finishing of her home a year later.

Melissa Krebeck

The third week after the storm Melissa's family was excited to have electricity back for three days. It would be another week before it was restored permanently. "It was wonderful for those three days," she recalled laughing. "The next week of not having power after the three days of having it was worse than initially after the storm," she shared. Melissa made the best of the situation, enjoyed her shaded front yard in the mornings and cleaning the shaded backyard in the afternoons. It took a while to clean-up the yard. "We did the little debris stuff, so I could hang up a clothes line," she explained.

266

The kids were back in school around the first part of November. "I think a lot of kids went back even before their houses had electricity because they could get two hot meals, breakfast and lunch, and they didn't have to wear their school uniforms until after Christmas" she shared. Melissa clarified that "it was a kind of come as you are and be here," situation. "They didn't have homework," she continued. Soon, Melissa was also able to return to working normal hours. "Working normal hours and having the children in school like normal, made up for the lack of normalcy in the rest of my life," she added. "But it's hard," she continued, "the boys are in Scouts and all the places we camp were affected by the hurricane." Melissa described how they couldn't camp at St. Andrews State Park or Florida Caverns State Park.

In September prior to the storm the local Boy Scout troops had a big camp out at the Florida Caverns State Park, which Melissa was thankful to have now cherished photos. "We had hiked into Caverns and had a day of doing skills building," she explained. "Then we had our court of honor that night, where the parents came," she continued. After they fed everyone "we got a special tour of the Caverns and then less than a month later, it will never be the same." "We had camped at St. Joseph Park and liked to go there as a family," she shared. "You can go to St. Andrews State Park, but up where we used to go swim on the ocean side, you can't swim, because there is no beach." she added. She clarified that the Gulf is beyond the dunes. "The scout troop camped there last May and they were able to get out but it was just different." "It's sad about the Chattahoochee State Park not reopening," she continued. "And people here are afraid to plant trees," Melissa added.

Boy Scouts enjoying camp out at Florida Caverns State Park in September 2018 just a couple of weeks before Hurricane Michael. Photos provided by Melissa Krebeck.

According to Melissa, her yard is about 90 percent cleaned-up. Like many she still has two root balls in her yard. "One is in the front and tangled up with City water lines, probably that stump will be there forever," she shared. Melissa and her neighbor had a pine tree that fell in between their homes. The way that it was laying required them to pay someone to remove it, because if it rolled it would damage one of the homes. "This company that came in was wonderful" she explained. "They came in, did the house across the street and then camped there," she continued. As the company worked removing trees throughout their neighborhood, Melissa found some security in knowing they were there. "You could hear the sirens," she explained. "The Saturday after the storm my mom and I had laid down to go to sleep, and a light shown in my window" she shared. "I jumped up and shined my light out the window and screamed 'what are you doing in my yard,'" she continued.

Melissa learned that it was the police, who were chasing someone through her backyard. "I think that is why my water got fixed as fast as it did, because the Police trudged through the swamp of my backyard," she added laughing. She explained that the broken pipe was pumping out a great deal of water. "The Fire Department had seen it when they were coming to check on houses, and I had called the City Public Works Department and left a message, but they were stretched so thin," she explained. "That happened Saturday night and I came home from church Sunday morning and the water line was fixed," she added laughing.

"The church just breaks my heart," Melissa expressed with a sigh. "I'm heart-broken over the state of Saint Lukes." "However, I'm grateful for the people," she continued. "I feel like we are closer as a family." After a long pause Melissa recalled how Saint Luke's Episcopal Church choir was singing and record number of people were in attendance the previous Sunday. "It's the shared experience that brings us closer," she continued, "and unless you have experienced it, you don't understand it."

Melissa moved to Marianna in 2007. "It wasn't too long before the storm that I had eaten at the Bistro . . .[Bistro Palms] . . . and I came up to the light and you could see the art museum and that little stretch" she continued, "and it's just such a pretty spot." "You had the trees from Confederate Park and we had such a pretty little town and it seems scarred." "And it is" she added. Melissa continued to express her thankfulness for trees around the courthouse. "We are starting to look more normalish," she continued. "We've had a huge influx of new people to the food pantry," Melissa explained. "There seems to be more displaced people, who are new to the food pantry," she continued, "and a lot of the people who used to come to the food pantry are simply gone." Melissa shared how there are people, she hasn't seen since the hurricane. "I'm assuming they just moved." Many of the indigent Melissa referred to did not have a home after the storm. The ones who were fortunate enough to live in a rental property, may have been displaced because the owners did not want to repair or replace the structure after Hurricane Michael came through Marianna. "That happened to a boy in my sons' scout troop," she added. The family Melissa referred to was renting, and after the storm there was no place for them to live. The mother asked her company to transfer her to Fort Walton Beach and they left.

"It's really a story of the haves and the have nots," she continued. "If you had the ways and the means, you're okay; if you didn't you're still struggling," Melissa explained.

Michelle Borden

For nearly four weeks Michelle commuted to work from Crawfordville to Marianna. "After one week I was like, I can't do this anymore," she explained. "I'd have to leave the house at 6:30 a.m. eastern time, and I got home at 6:30 p.m. eastern time." Melissa was able to take advantage of a commuter car in Tallahassee that was helpful for her.

Michelle's boyfriend was called to work the day after the children left. He worked and stayed in Pensacola for two weeks. After that he was laid off. He took her father's chainsaw and returned to help people in Marianna. "Every time we went by the house, we would salvage something," she shared. There were sentimental things they couldn't save that Michelle had hoped to give to her children one day, including a photo of her grandfather at is first communion, her autobiography she wrote in the eighth grade, a photo of her at age four, her birth certificate, and a file her mother kept of her achievements growing up. Michelle recalled how there were many days when she'd go to get something and realize it was gone. Also, overtime Michelle would be so overwhelmed by the house when she'd go there that she would ask herself if it was really important. Not only was going into the home traumatic, but she did not have the space to save everything. She remembered having a cabinet full of arts and crafts in her home that she loved. "I had all the scissors with the fun little cutting styles," she continued. She had every CD she had owned as an adult. "We went to the Rainforest Café for one of my birthday's and I still had the glass that I'd never taken out of the box because one day I was going to have a shelf where I could put everything up," she added. "All the stuff and clutter that I had in my life was now gone," she stated sadly.

Michelle was able to salvage most of the belongings in the kitchen. They were able to take a table and chairs set that she had purchased for $70 off of Craig's List. However, her brand new refrigerator that was ruined by the storm, which she continues to make payments on. Similarly, she still had to pay for the new sofa that was destroyed.

Michelle and her boyfriend stayed in Crawfordville for about three weeks. When the children returned, she would have to commute with the children so they could go to school. Michelle explained how her son would sleep during the commute and stay up all night. She negotiated with the insurance company about money for renting while her home was being rebuilt, and she was able to move back to Marianna. They agreed to pay for her rental for one year with furnishings for the house. They had to get rental furniture for every room except the kitchen. "It wasn't the best," she explained. Although uncomfortable and unattractive, she was thankful to have something.

The insurance company came out twenty days after the storm. The adjuster explained to Michelle that he couldn't total the house until she removed the tree. "I was like, which one?" she shared. After the adjuster left Michelle called the insurance company and shared digital photos of her home, "and the representative said 'this is a total –I don't know what the problem is!'" Michelle continued. The adjuster returned and started taking photos inside the home. "We got the check around Thanksgiving." she added. "Then, of course, you have to send it to the mortgage company and they send you a portion back and that whole process" she continued. The home was demolished by early January. Then, they picked a floor plan and began working towards their new home. They finalized the house in February 2019, almost five months after the storm. When she got the check for the property in February, she paid off all the credit card debt and began picking out new furniture for the children's room, living room and her bedroom. Then, she returned the rental furniture. They had the final meeting in February and plans were to break ground in April. However, the groundbreaking was a month later.

Meanwhile she was traveling with her job to Yazoo, Mississippi in January, April and June. The latest trip in September was to Montgomery. In November she will have to return to Mississippi. While she is away, the children stay with their father. This is all because of damage related to Hurricane Michael.

The house sat for two months with no work being done on it. She described all types of contractor and subcontractor issues. Contractors and subcontractors in Marianna are booked out for years in the future. They are attempting to work on too many jobs at one time. "Originally, they told me the house would be done by now," she continued. "I should be moving into my new house right now and I'm not!" The completion date has been moved out to November. The insurance will pay for her rental until October 31st, which is not long enough. As bad as this sounds, her insurance company was great compared to other stories that have been shared.

Shelby Durham

Matthew and Shelby lived with his parents for about five months. "We were able to find a rental house one block from Matt's parents," she recalled. "They were super excited because I found out two weeks to the day after Hurricane Michael hit that I was pregnant," she added.

Shelby expressed how much the town has improved. "I'm thankful to see the buildings being put back together, like the end of Winn Dixie, Wells Fargo and that part of the building above the Art Factory," she explained. "I'm thankful to see the town being pieced back together and I feel like we've done a lot in a year" she continued. "We've done a ton in a year." "It was hard to see the town so beaten" she added. "I don't know if I will even see the trees back to what they were in my lifetime," she explained. "I think there is a sense of unity since the storm." Shelby shared how she's been gathering keepsakes for her son, who went through the storm before being born.

James Lash

Once Ronnie and Debbie's power was restored, James and Catherine Lash moved in with them. On Christmas Eve, James fell and broke his hip and had to have hip replacement surgery. Debbie took care of her mother and father during this time. James was determined to get better and move back home. However, they wouldn't be able to move into their new manufactured home for eight months.

Photos provided by Debbie Lash Lollie.

James explained how he was able to save the dryer. James' house had tongue in grove cypress paneling. He explained, "when the house came down the cypress paneling was like a box supporting part of the living room, only the living room collapsed inside of it." Before the home was demolished, two of James' nieces from Texas went into the dilapidated structure and saved his family photographs. "I told them I thought I'd kill you, but I thank you," he expressed thankfully. "When the two girls said they were coming, I told them no food, no beds, no place to stay," he continued. "But when they come they brought food, money and supplies," he shared. "They was a lifesaver for me." James shared the nieces were in Chipley the next d ay, and that is when they saved some other item.

FEMA offered James a travel trailer at one point, "but when they got there they said they couldn't put it there because of the lot width was only 65 feet," he shared. "I have the biggest lot on the street" he continued. James' home is in a subdivision platted in 1946. He shared how they offered him another travel trailer, but the wheel chair ramp and doorways were not wide enough to accommodate the needs of his bedridden wife.

While his insurance company didn't pay for everything, James was able to design his own home with colors and furnishings to suit him. He was able to design the floor plan with a large closet in the room where Catherine stays so he could store the hoist and wheel chair. Then, James shopped around for used furniture. Everything in his living room he bought new. The most important piece of furniture James bought was his recliner. "If it don't match, big deal," he shared. "How many people come to see you when you get to be 90 years old." Now, James is happy in his new home.

The Lash family's new manufactured home. Photo provided by Debbie Lash Lollie.

James Lash expressed how he thought it would be at least three or four more years before the town had a sense of normalcy. He explained how people have lost jobs and left. "Nobody can believe that it was still that high a category 70 miles off the beach!"

Ronstance Pittman

She returned to work after electricity had been restored. Ronstance explained that her job is a luxury for people. "A fitness trainer was the last thing people were thinking about," she continued. Her business didn't get back to normal until January. So, their income was affected.

According to Ronstance everything is back to normal for the family. Her husband's truck didn't get repaired, so there is a dent and a leak when it rains. They replaced the carport. All the trees in the area are gone. She remembered how beautiful the scenery had been previously.

Among the many things she did in her role as the Jackson County NAACP President, she advocated for residents that were given 48 hours to relocate from their apartments. Although not successful that time, she was successful later at another apartment complex in having the police there to inform tenants of their rights and extending their time to relocate. At another apartment complex she received a call that everyone had power around them, but they didn't have any power. She asked Florida Public Utilities to come out and their power was restored. In another situation, a couple was renting a house where a tree fell in the house and the landlord wouldn't repair it.. Ronstance helped them.

Dom's Mobile Hut and Blue Magic ISP

According to Dominic Garcia, owner of Dom's Mobile Hut and Blue Magic ISP, Blue Magic was the first Internet provider that was up. "We went business to business here in Marianna selling our Internet boxes," he explained. His sales associate Torro Duncan explained how he was able to get into the Mexico

Beach area after Hurricane Michael because he and his family owned a beach house there. "We probably got 400 to 500 customers between Wewahitchka, Port Saint Joe and Mexico Beach," Torro shared. This not only helped people have access to information, but it helped Dominic's company start up.

Torro left his home in Altha that was destroyed by Hurricane Michael to help others. He lost 80 trees on a three acre tract and is still living in a FEMA trailer. Torro was not alone. Dominic has only recently returned to his home. Sixteen of the 24 trees that fell on his property landed on his house. Yet, he set out to help others after the storm.

Penello's Italian Cuisine

While the Pinello family were delayed in their plans, they continued to move forward with opening their restaurant. Finally, in August 2019, almost a year later, they were able to open for business. The new restaurant provided additional options in the community and helped with the rebuilding process.

Wells Fargo

Cynthia Zubia clarified all the work that went to making sure the branch remained open throughout the period of reconstruction and recovery. One of the first things Wells Fargo did was open a drive-thru and use a trailer as a remote branch in the same parking lot. When it was really hot, the City of Marianna allowed Wells Fargo to use their building to accommodate the needs of their customers. The company deployed a mobile response unit to Marianna right after the storm that went to the Panama City location with a remote team to Marianna to help service customers with their banking needs throughout the Panhandle. "Anyone who was impacted by Hurricane Michael would be able to utilize those services, which was a phenomenal experience," she shared. They did a lot of different things to support their employees during the recovery period to make it possible for them to come to work and be comfortable and sustained. It allowed them to work without being concerned about what they were going through personally and receive the support they needed at work.

Cynthia went on to share how after the hurricane, Wells Fargo donated a million dollars to Hurricane Michael relief efforts, including funds to the American Red Cross and local nonprofits in the affected communities. Some funding was provided to the Chipola Area Habitat for Humanity to build new houses and help with home repairs. They also donated money to the Consortium of Education Foundation, and the Jackson and Washington Education Foundations. They are glad to be part of the community.

Photo provided by Wells Fargo.

Jackie added, "Wells Fargo was also able to support student activities." While families were still going through the recovery process, they helped support graduation trips, graduation expenses, eyeglasses, college application fees, fees for attendance to educational summer camps, school supplies, individual student's needs, such as clothing and hygiene items. This assistance was invaluable to families who were devastated by the storm and unforeseen financial crisis.

The mural was actually designed by a dedicated team of graphic artists. Similar murals can be seen in other branches in other parts of the country. There is a mural key that is installed along with the mural that describes each image that's featured. Armstrong Purdee is one of the historical people represented in the mural. He was Jackson County's first African American lawyer. The selection of Mr. Purdee was made after working with the local historical society, through libraries and historical archives. According to Jackie Kendall, Wells Fargo gathered information from these resources "to reflect the history and diversity of our community." This is appropriate in the recovery of Marianna, because Hurricane Michael broke down walls and everyone worked together.

While it seems slow, the community continues to rebuild structures and hope through steady progress that is sometimes not so easy to see. Patience is difficult when living among the rubble and after losing so much. Would the town find any hope?

PART VI

Did Anything Positive Come from Hurricane Michael?

Y‌ou may ask yourself could anything positive come from the destruction and devastation of Hurricane Michael. While this may seem hard to believe, the answer is yes. I call it the silver lining to the thunder cloud. How can good come from bad, and happy from sad? The City of Marianna found rainbows among the rubble. Sunrises provided hope that in helping others another day, their own lives would be so much better. At the end of each day the lack of the natural environment loved by so many would provide visibility to beautifully painted sunsets and the hope. While everyone still loved their luxury items, they learned that their love for God, family and neighbors was much stronger. What could be better than happiness after the storm in a small rural town?

Chapter Eleven

The Silver Lining

When you have lost everything around you that you feel like you need for survival, you are forced to figure out what is most important in your life. Maybe it is not your car or your house. Maybe you can learn to live without Internet, telephone and electricity. After all people have lived happily for many generations without cars, houses, cell phones and electricity. That's when you learn that the ones you love are more important than all of those things.

Mayor Williams

Mayor Williams explained "the regard for human life and the lives that were spared ended up being more important than material things." That is what people were focused on. "With all the devastation going on you rarely heard people walking around talking about my house, and my this and my that." "They were in help mode trying to restore things." "It wasn't a pity party," he shared. Mayor Williams recalled people coming together trying to get things done, and the opportunity for new beginnings. He remembered that there were people who couldn't get jobs before, who were able to get jobs after the storm. "That was an economic boost that helped deter crime because when people get desperate they tend to resort to something else," Mayor Williams explained. He remembered that crime was less than normal. To Mayor Williams establishing the curfew was worth more than all the help we received from other places.

Corporal Mears

Mike explained that he had made new friends and become closer with the people he works with at the Sheriff's Department. Positive fellowship with those he works with was his silver lining.

Kenny Griffin

Kenny shared several silver lining stories. One was people his family didn't know, who came to their home and gave them a travel trailer and a 50 gallon drum of gasoline. Kenny Griffin recalled stories his parents told about World War II and the unification of the nation, which was essentially about the welfare of the individual. "After the storm there was no government to help you," he continued. "People had to rely on self, and after that there was the people coming over the hill with church organizations," he added. Hurricane Michael taught us our worth. "If I had a hundred dollar bill and you had five gallons of gas, the gas had more value," Kenny continued. "The bad part about living rural is rural, and the good part about living rural is we all had chainsaws," Kenny explained. "So, we had to help each other without waiting on anyone," he added. Kenny explained that he did not know about people setup in town providing free food and supplies, because there were no communications. They only thing people knew was what we could do for each other.

The people in Marianna and Jackson County have a lot of pride and don't like to ask for help. People Kenny didn't even know donated supplies for him to distribute in a manner that the locals could accept. Individuals who didn't have anything were helping others, because it was the right thing to do. It was a bad time, but so much good came out. "It was bad with all the destruction and loss, but good in all that recognized what and who was important," Kenny shared. "The nicest thing was the first time hot shower," Kenny recalled. The town has learned to appreciate the smallest things in life.

Carmen Smith

Carmen described how one of the good things that came from Hurricane Michael was the sense of unity. "Hurricane Michael moved us forward," she shared. The opportunity is available to expand housing and build capacity so that long term there will be sustained growth. "I'm hoping with the funding that will trickle down, that there will be some things put in place to improve the quality of life for our residents," Carmen added. "I believe there may have been an uptick in economic spending locally, which is good," she continued.

John Milton

Seventh generation resident and business owner, John Milton had hurricane damage at home and at his rental properties. Despite the destruction, he shared how he felt blessed. John's optimistic attitude and love for the community led him to conclude that for those who choose, there is an opportunity for growth. He not only chose to take advantage of the opportunity for growth, but decided to promote the community and help others. John upgraded his car wash in town and is donating a portion of the earnings to community youth groups.

Jay James

Jay shared that from the very beginning her beauty pageant friends, other friends and family brought her family fuel, money and supplies. She felt blessed by her friends and family, and by her aunt, who allowed them to stay with her. "I saw God all over the place, working everywhere, as everything was falling into place," Jay explained. She recalled how they would take two steps forward and four back along their journey. "Our blessing was we built our dream home" and the events over the year "brought us closer together," she added. Jay shared how Hurricane Michael had renewed her faith in God. Jay went on to express how much she loves this community, because of the importance placed on family.

Melissa Krebeck

Melissa had been recently divorced and after the storm her life changed. "I just decided to have a life rather than waiting for a life to happen," she shared. Melissa met someone and her life has changed for the better. "I do more and get out more," she continued. "I eat dinner with friends." She also became more active at church, joining the choir, singing solos and becoming involved with the church youth ministry. Melissa's neighborhood has continued to be friendly since Hurricane Michael. "It's not just the adults either," Melissa added. "The children have grown closer and hang out together all the time."

Melissa continued, "recently, they had a potluck dinner in commemoration of their survival and newly found friendships".

Melissa loves how the community came together after the storm and looked out for one another. "We have this long term recovery group, which is really doing good things," Melissa shared. One lady Melissa knew from the food pantry expressed how the United Methodist Committee on Relief (UMCOR), working through the North Florida Inland Long Term Recovery Group, had repaired her home to a livable condition and provided her with new furnishings.

Melissa's son Zachary was confirmed the Sunday after the storm as previously planned. "I was so happy the bishop did that," she added. "It meant a lot." Her house faired-well. Melissa's big tree in her front yard took out her water line, but on the City of Marianna's side, so she did not have to pay for maintenance. Now that all Melissa's trees are gone, she has grass for the first time.

Michelle Borden

Although Michelle and her family went through a horrible experience, there were positive things that happened along the way. First, Michelle's house was built in 1955 and now she will have a new home. Michelle explained that the bathrooms were pink and green, and needed updating. Another thing that made a huge difference was Michelle commuted in the mornings from the eastern time zone to the central time zone. While she would arrive home late, she did not have to get up as early as if it had been the opposite. Also, she commuted away from the sun both ways. A fourth positive thing was she drove 45 minutes to the commuter vehicle, where the commuters took turns driving.

They would alternate who was driving. Additionally, this saved Michelle money on her leased vehicle because the mileage going back and forth would have been very costly. Sixth, Michelle's children had a great time at their grandparent's home and she still was able to video chat with them as much as she wanted. They were also able to go to three different Halloween events. Halloween was cancelled in Marianna. Another silver lining was a few months before the storm Michelle had taken a photo of the photo of herself at age four and made a side-by-side posting with her son, because they looked so much alike. Although the original photo was lost, it was saved in a digital format. Michelle also explained that the storage off her carport did not receive significant damage. In the storage room, Michelle had three totes of memorabilia that survived. While Michelle and her family lost almost everything, two weeks after the storm she received boxes of clothes. "Someone even sent me a snow suit," she shared. Whatever she didn't need, she passed along to others.

Paula Livergood

Paula learned how to be more prepared. "I learned how to cook breakfast on the grill and that there is a lot of good in people regardless to how much our society has declined," she shared. "There are so many ways you can help people," she continued. "Just because you are one person doesn't mean you can't help," Paula added. "Even if you just have a little, it all adds up and helps people," she continued. "Makes me want to help others in the future by going physically with supplies" she continued. Paula recalled helping after Hurricane Katrina by sending clothes and supplies. "Seeing how much the public gave us, makes me more proud to be an American and more determined to help others," she shared. "I wish I could thank every single person

who brought food, supplies, cooked or donated from their homes
to help us."

Shelby Durham

Shelby shared that Hurricane Michael opened doors for her
husband to start his own paint and body shop. The success of
Matthew's business provided Shelby the opportunity stay home
with her baby, which she shared, would have never been option
when they lived in Panama City. "It's been a huge blessing" she
continued. "Hurricane Michael put Matthew and I back where
we were supposed to be" she added.

Ronnie Keel

After the storm Ronnie and his neighbors became closer and
looked out for one another. "I had a bunch of deer meat in the
freezer and after I got the cooker up and going, I fixed sausage for
the neighbors and people around working." In fact, that is what
I was doing when I heard that Royce's house was on fire."
Ronnie's friend, Jimmy Standland, had gone to the shelter to ride
out the storm and stayed there a few days. While Jimmie was
away Ronnie looked out for Jimmy's place.

James Lash

James Lash had always wanted a big screen television. After
Christmas he bought one that was fifty percent off. He was also
able to purchase a new recliner of his choice. The biggest silver
lining for James was in the things his family did to help him, and
being able to move into a new home with his wife.

Marianna Truss and Marianna Metal Roofing

Prior to Hurricane Michael the owners of Marianna Truss and Marianna Metal Roofing, Garry and Debbie Gochenaur had been expanded their twenty year old business to include a furniture line. Hurricane Michael was hard on the Gochenaur family, which had two pregnant ladies in the home the day the hurricane made landfall. One was due on October 13th.

While they had storm damage, Hurricane Michael provided opportunities for the business. Garry and Debbie began feeding their crew at work, so they could worker later. This would go on for months as they did whatever they could to make metal roofing available as soon as possible for the community. The owners found the company to be doing four times the work previously done. Then, they purchased additional equipment, delivery trucks and dumpsters. Then, to further expedite production, Garry purchased metal from a national supplier.

On May 7, 2019 Marianna Truss and Marianna Metal Roofing annexed into the City of Marianna and expanded by thirteen acres. This was opportunity for City and business growth.

Wells Fargo

The mural at Wells Fargo was tasteful and classy with how it relates to our community. It represented big business to small town. It helps restore the integrity of our downtown. "Instead of tearing the building down and building another fancy building, or even packing up and moving on, Wells Fargo rebuilt," Commissioner Williams shared. "I really felt blessed to be a part of that ribbon cutting."

Even under the worst of circumstances some of the residents who had the worst devastation saw good in the bad. Was it a question of an optimistic personality versus a pessimistic personality? I think it was more than that. After interviewing more than 100 people about Hurricane Michael from diverse settings, I found that while the people in Marianna loved the beautiful natural environment, warm summer nights, huge oaks with moss hanging down, historic downtown and their memories of all these places, that was not the only thing that made Marianna special. The best thing about Marianna wasn't a thing, but the people. Despite all the destruction of Hurricane Michael, survivors were still the same people they were before the hurricane, only better. The shared devastation and recovery has brought people closer together. It's a blessing to be part of this wonderful community!

PART VII

MY STORY

While writing this book, I was also living in the community. I experienced the storm, devastation, loss and relived the stories shared with me many times. I can hear the voices and remember the tears of the many people who took time to speak with me while I was preparing this book. One might think I would be saddened by all the depressing stories. Quite the opposite was true. I listened carefully, relived the events of every story with the story teller and understood their pain, suffering, fear, depression and hope for the future. What a blessing it has been for me to have this opportunity. While I listened, I was involved in cleanup and recovery at home and work.

If you haven't already noticed, there is overlap in the stories. That is one of the best parts of living in a small town. My father is Ronnie Keel and his neighbor is James Lash. Royce Reagan was my teacher, and has been a great friend and mentor. The majority of the first responders and people representing businesses and organizations mentioned are colleagues. I enjoy working with them and calling them my friends. I am a member of Saint Luke's Episcopal Church. I love the members and call them my family. I also enjoy visiting other churches and have become friends with Reverend Mizer and Kevin Yoder. I met some of the people interviewed for the first time when they walked through my door. Yet, I found their stories usually overlapped with someone else I had interviewed or knew. Before they left my office, I felt a bond with them, as well. Like everyone I spoke with, I feel blessed to have survived Hurricane Michael.

I was sitting in church on October 13, 2019, over a year after the storm. Father David was preaching on gratitude.

> "To practice gratitude intentionally changes a person's life, to be sure. It also changes the character of a congregation. When Christians practice gratitude, they come to worship 'not just to get something out of it,' but to give thanks and praise God.. . . . I think gratitude is the noblest emotion."[5]

As I listened, I realized the community had practiced gratitude. Everyone was so thankful just to have survived Hurricane Michael. Perhaps this was a result of them coming together to help one another, not just one day, but day after day for more than a year. If gratitude is a noble emotion, this community must be among the noblest of which to reside and be a part.

---

[5] From "Sermon on Luke 17:11-19, Proper 23, Year C, 2019," by Father David Green. Reprinted with permission.

Chapter Twelve
At Home

fter work on Monday, October 8th I was excited to be in route for my scheduled salon appointment. It's a time I enjoy sharing stories with my hair stylist and sweet friend, Necia. There had been talk at work that day about a storm in the Gulf of Mexico, but I was busy and just didn't pay too much attention. Some of the ladies at work were panicking and I told them it was no big deal. At the salon I heard more of the same concerns. While I still didn't think it was anything to be overly concerned about, I listened. Then, I promptly told everyone that the storm headed our way was like so many others I'd seen and they should relax.

By Tuesday morning the weather still didn't look too serious. Before leaving for work I had a discussion with my husband about securing everything in the yard. Then, I went to work as usual. Whenever there is a storm coming through, I always secure the office. My staff assisted me in ensuring window sills were clear, papers were put away, and picture frames were lying flat so not to fall. Later in the day the City Manager notified all the department heads that City Hall would be closed on Wednesday, October 10, 2018, but we would return the following day. The doors were posted with the same information. On breaks my staff filled up their cars with fuel, and picked up water, food and supplies.

Our son-in-law, Tim, would be required to work during the hurricane, so I had made arrangements for our daughter, Anna, and grandson, Landon, to stay with us. Our older child, Trey, lives and works in Tallahassee, and was unable to join us. Before leaving work I ordered a couple of pizzas. Then, I made my way to the grocery store to pick up a few supplies. That's when I found bare shelves and lines of people all the way to the back of the store. I turned around and saw Charlotte Green. I said "pff, it's not worth it!" Then, I headed over to KFC and picked up a bucket of chicken. I figured between the pizza and chicken, we were covered. I couldn't have been more wrong about what was to take place.

We enjoyed family time that evening, while what suddenly looked like the most beautiful storm I'd ever seen was shown on television radars. Ashley, City of Marianna Code Enforcement Officer, sent me a text sharing how her daughters were frightened. I encouraged her to tell them about how the storm images were unique and calm them with scientific information about the storm. By this time I thought the storm would be significant, but I never dreamed it would be devastating. Our family had ridden out Hurricane Opal in 1995 in a mobile home. I remembered the mobile home rocked, but we were only without electricity for a day or so. While I knew I didn't want to be in a mobile home, I felt fairly safe in our brick house.

Wednesday morning Hurricane Michael was much stronger. It was predicted to be a category three or four hurricane. Later we learned that the storm was headed directly toward Marianna and might be a category five hurricane. In the back of my mind I still thought it might weaken. That was typically what happened as a storm made landfall. The land would break the storm up, and it would weaken substantially before it arrived 70 miles inland. My mother and sister evacuated for Tennessee that morning. My mom's last request was for me to check on my father, because he was at home alone. This would be a promise I couldn't keep.

Our front porch has a store front window that provides a great view, but also could be a weak spot on the house. So, my husband, Britt, moved his truck in front of the window to help block the wind. Then, he walked around the perimeter of our parcel and prayed the blood of Jesus. This, without a doubt, spared our lives and home. We continued to watch the weather reports. In the early afternoon the wind and storms picked up. Then, we observed as the local weather station went off the air. From that moment forward it was difficult to access information. Not long afterwards we would lose electricity and phone service. Our family moved to the front porch to watch the weather from the safety of our home. Once the eye wall was upon us, there were white-out conditions where it was difficult to see past arm's length distance. I setup pillows in an internal hall and played games with my grandson. My husband and daughter continued to watch the storm. Anna would soon join me.

During the eye of the storm, we stepped outside briefly to peruse the damage, which was significant. However, we would find the worst part of the storm had not arrived yet. I called my father, who told me his neighbor's bedridden wife had rain pouring in on her. The neighbor's house was destroyed. He was talking about James Lash. After I hung up, I immediately called my colleague, the Fire Chief, to see if help could be sent for her. That's when I learned that first responders were unable to respond due to the number of fallen trees on all the roadways. I had always listened to recommendations to evacuate and knew the reasons behind the pleas, but I never experienced the "aha moment" until that day.

When the eye wall started coming over us again, we were all sitting on the porch. At that point we went into the master bedroom closet, which was a tight space, to ride out the storm. It's in those moments that you can't tell what's happening in the world. You are isolated and without information. You can't see anything and you don't know when it is safe to come out.

After the storm had passed, we went outside to see devastation. Our huge oak trees were twisted up like the twist lollipops I bought as a kid. The sight was beyond description. The privacy fence around our swimming pool was mangled and fallen trees were covering our yard. We had some flooding in our family room and some problems with our well. However, we were all safe and our home was still standing.

Our grandson Landon, age four, helping with cleanup. Photo provided by Anna Dennis Gilley.

Britt was able to hook up our generator and we ran a few electrical devices at a time. This was wonderful, because it was so hot and humid after the storm. We had a small window air conditioning unit in our family room that provided relief from the heat. We could watch television, but couldn't see the local news. There was little information available on the national news. We didn't have Internet or land-line phones. Cellular service would come and go. At some point our son-in-law was able to contact our daughter. That's when we began to learn about some of the damage in other areas. We still didn't begin to know how extensive the damage was.

One thing we did have was water. Britt was able to repair our well and we enjoyed cold showers. Despite ice cold showers, it was nice to be clean and be able to flush the toilet, especially when it was so hot outside. We also had a grill that never moved during the storm. Britt, the supreme chef, cooked nice meals in our cast iron cookware on the grill. One night he had cooked us the most delicious shepherd's pie I've ever tasted. I felt tremendous guilt for eating it, when I knew others had less.

The isolation we experienced was like nothing I had gone through in my life. We had each other and were thankful. Yet, we didn't know what was going on around us. Britt's parents live next door. So, we were able to check on them and them on us. We could see what was in front of us, but nothing beyond. I could sometimes receive texts from my mother pleading with me to notify her of our safety, but couldn't respond.

At some point on Friday Tim was able to return home with reports regarding damage where he worked and along the way. Our supplies were low, so we knew we needed to venture out. Friday afternoon the five of us loaded up not really knowing where to go. We had heard Old US Road South was impassable, so we took Berkshire to Caverns Road. As we turned onto Berkshire we could not see a road. All we could see was fallen trees and massive destruction. This was worse than what I had thought. For some reason I felt similarly to what Wilanne had described as the storm only wreaking havoc on my street. We turned around and went north on Old US Road, which had fallen power poles, power lines and trees everywhere. We were able to make our way down a narrow path, where in some cases power poles were hanging over the road. Then, we turned west toward US231. The people in this rural area had cleared a narrow pathway and cars were waiting in line to pass. Once we made it to US 231, we drove down a completely cleared road to Dothan. It took about three to four hours to make what was normally a 45 minute drive. Then, we began a search to find fuel.

Meanwhile, I was able to obtain a cellular signal. I contacted the fire chief who told me to stay home. He explained how people were having wrecks and there was no place to take those with injuries. I was able to check in with my mother, who was still trying to make contact with my brother. I called my friend, Lotus, who was trapped on her farm with her teenage daughter. I was able to contact Trey, who was aggravated about the power loss. Trey was otherwise fine. I was able to make contact with Ashley Bradie from my office. She told me about the damage in Marianna, which gave me a better sense of what was going on around us. She also let us know where we could go for fuel. I was also able to touch base with the City Manager, who instructed me to not return to the office. He shared that City Hall was locked up due to some looting in town. This was very frustrating to me, because I wanted to help. However, I heeded their warnings and didn't return to work. Britt was able to call Wal-Mart, where he works as a Department Manager. He was only able to get a recording saying the store was closed.

When we arrived at the gas station, there was a line of cars waiting to purchase fuel that was sold in limited amounts with cash only. Still, this would help keep the refrigerator and freezer running. Then, we made our way back to our home. By this time it was dark and hard to maneuver through the narrow paths between fallen trees. Driving conditions were beyond dangerous. It was also after curfew. There was a fear that we would be stopped and not allowed to return home. What started out as an afternoon drive for fuel lasted probably eight hours.

Saturday, we made our way back north of Dothan to buy food and other supplies that we needed with a credit card. Not taking the hurricane seriously also meant that I didn't have much cash. We did not know food and supplies were being brought in to Marianna. Lack of information was one of the worst parts of the experience. While we were away, the City Manager, Jim Dean, called me. He had made it to my house to check on my family. Jim shared that I needed to contact my staff to report to work on Monday. I was able to contact each one. When I called Paula Livergood, Planning Tech for the City of Marianna, I learned that her home was in bad shape and vehicle was destroyed.

While we were out, my husband called and found out that he could return to work on Monday, as well. This was good news because we were unsure if he still had a job. When he returned he saw the skylights and air conditioning units ripped off the top of the building. Britt reported a layaway trailer had been thrown into the woods, and several trailers had roofs torn off. Hurricane Michael had blown the doors off the grocery side of the building and debris was scattered all over the store. The garden center patio roof had been ripped off. There was approximately $20 million in damage, mainly merchandise in a business that employees about 300 people in the area. A Cotton Team, professional cleanup team, was brought in to help and the store reopened a week after the storm.

Around the same time that Britt and I returned to work, Tim reported in to the National Guard. Anna and Landon stayed at our home during the day, while we were working for a couple of months. Their presence helped maintain some security so that our generator was not stolen. Plus, it gave them a cool place to be after the storm.

A few days following the storm a group came through who offered to remove our fallen oak trees for $15 thousand each. We had several trees down, but six to eight huge oaks that were twisted in ways that are difficult to explain. It would be a few months before the trees were removed. My husband took down several, which concerned me greatly. One of our neighbors died when he was cleaning up debris and a tree rolled over on him. My husband's parents helped with the removal of a couple of the trees that were hard to reach. Slowly we were able to repair our fence, which still needs some repairs.

We began noticing structures in the day and lights at night that we had never seen before. The natural buffer of vegetation that we all loved was gone. On the other hand, we started noticing the most beautiful sunrises, sunsets, and rainbows. The colors were more vibrant than any I'd ever seen.

On Monday nights I traveled about twenty miles west to Chipley to meet with some friends for Bible study. Chipley wasn't spared from the devastation. I listened to my friends share their experiences. My Aunt Pat lives in Chipley, and she had to live with my cousin John for several months, while my cousin Tracy helped her with clean up and repairs. For months I would pass Circle D Ranch on the way to and from Chipley and see debris burning non-stop.

After the first of the year we had a new surprise. Anna and Tim announced that they were expecting a baby. Grandchildren must be the best silver lining anyone could ever want. While our lives were extremely busy with recovery at home and work, we waited with anticipation for our new granddaughter who arrived on September 3, 2019.

Our grandchildren, Kara and Landon. Photo provided by Anna Gilley.

When you are busy, time flies and memories fade. Much of the remainder of the year seems like a blur. Our historic church still has not been repaired, but we have become closer as a congregation while waiting. We daily pass areas destroyed by Hurricane Michael and gasp. I look around sadly and reminisce about what once was a beautiful historic town. It hurts my heart. Yet, I look forward to helping the town rebuild even better.

SURVIVING HURRICANE MICHAEL: A COMMUNITY'S STORY OF DEVASTATION, SURVIVAL AND HOPE DURING RECOVERY

Top: Our Harlequin Great Dane, Singer running through the debris. **Bottom:** Our son-in-law, Tim and grandson, Landon. **Below**: Landon at Turner's Landing after Hurricane Michael. Photos provided by Anna Gilley.

Chapter Thirteen

In the Municipal Development Department

Monday morning, October 15, 2019, I realized how spoiled and high maintenance I had become. I took a cold shower and tried to put on makeup that dripped off my face with the sweat that kept accumulating. I couldn't dry my hair because the generator could only run a limited number of appliances at a time, and I had a high powered blow dryer. I felt ugly, but picked up Paula and reported to work. There we began having daily meetings. My department's first task was to get our office ready to function. Then, we were assigned debris and brick removal by hand from the streets, sidewalks and parks. My assistant was assigned to work at the Emergency Operations Center answering phones.

Jackson Hospital fed us breakfast every morning, and people from all over the country brought lunch, which was available in different locations around town. Florida Public Utilities fed us lunch on a couple occasions and provided snacks for us to take. This was important because workers couldn't drive up to McDonalds and grab a burger. Everything was closed. This was something I had never really thought about before Hurricane Michael.

Soon after we began cleaning up debris, we saw that three ladies were not going to be able to make much progress without any equipment. We cleaned one park as best we could, while people came out of a nearby apartment complex to watch us. Clay Wells had offered his Kubota for us to use to haul off debris. Instead, we found locations where there were supplies and delivered them into the neighborhoods. On one of these delivery days, Chief Hayes Baggett requested I write a book on Hurricane Michael and I agreed.

At work we were provided hotspots, which I was allowed to use for my school work at home, since we still didn't have Internet or cellular service. The National Guard provided a huge satellite dish in the City Hall parking lot to assist with Internet access at work.

Left: Ashley Bradie, and me delivering food and water. **Right**: Ashley Bradie. Notice her beautiful smile. It felt good to help others. Photos provided by Paula Livergood who was riding in the trailer.

Going to work felt like joining the community. Returning home felt like isolation. By the following week I had discovered and adapted to the new normal routine. I think this probably happens to everyone. One thing I was glad to learn was how to dry my hair in the dark. We made adjustments in our life to make what was the new normal work. It would be 21 days after Hurricane Michael before our electrical power was restored. The first hot shower was amazing!

We were continually being charged for a landline phone service at home, which is where we received the Internet. To date I don't think it has been restored on our street. In February, we purchased new cellular phones with a new Internet provider, so we could have phone and Internet service. This was nearly five months after the storm.

Almost a year prior to the Hurricane Michael I had purchased a ticket to go to the Joyce Meyer Love Life Women's Conference in Tampa. I was blessed to have found someone to accompany me, but then we had the storm. I tried to cancel, but the hotel wouldn't release me from my reservations. So, my friend Peggy and I went to Tampa. The entire trip I was singing and having fun, and she was concerned about the storm. I kept reassuring her. When we arrived in Tampa, we had good food, air conditioned rooms, cellular and Internet services, and hot showers. It was amazing! Then, we worshipped God with about 10,000 other women. Wow! Good music and fun times.

SURVIVING HURRICANE MICHAEL: A COMMUNITY'S STORY OF DEVASTATION, SURVIVAL AND HOPE DURING RECOVERY

Me taking photos for insurance purposes at the MERE Complex .Photo provided by Paula Livergood

I was living in a false reality. When we returned home on Saturday evening about 8 p.m., I told my husband "I've got to run up to the store and pick up something". He replied that I couldn't do it. Being particularly stubborn, I went anyway. I found all the stores were closed except for Tom Thumb, which was surrounded by the NYPD. Marianna was in a police state and I was out after curfew. That's when reality set in. I guess I had been in shock, or possibly denial, before this point in time.

We returned to our church the next day, which was standing, but had issues. I remember thinking it would be nice, if I could just find some resemblance of normalcy somewhere. I'm still looking. Welcome to the new normal! The roads were piled ten or more feet high with debris. Driving had to be done with care because debris hauling trucks and people with signs directing traffic were in the road everywhere. You also had to maneuver carefully around lineman trucks.

During the first few days back at work, I had called some of the cities who had been impacted by Hurricane Ivan. I was told to get ready because I would be working day and night. I didn't see it. In fact, I still felt like I was contributing enough to cleanup efforts. I took an agenda item before the Mariana City Commission requesting some allowances for a temporary period of time. I requested the allowance of additional signage. I asked for homeowner reconstruction and roofing be allowed while permitting took place. Another need was for the allowance of living in RVs, using RVs for businesses and using pods during recovery. I suggested removing all development order fees and 17 percent of permitting fees to help with costs related to rebuilding. Finally, I asked for relaxation of code enforcement measures. It was approved and provided some relief for area residents and businesses. I felt like this was one way I was able to make a difference for the community, especially when it was difficult to find where a business was located or if it was open.

By Halloween conditions were not much better. Halloween was cancelled in Marianna by the City Commission, because of obvious dangers. A few groups got together and had a Halloween event at a local park. I never thought I would see the day when Halloween was cancelled. At work we kept busy and had an increase in permits. It would be January before we knew how busy we were going to be.

By January we were realizing a 470 percent increase in permitting, which has only slowed up slightly. Mostly due to the number of contractors in the area to do the work. One contractor explained how he is booked up until 2021. The building official was working day and night, and so were we. I decided to help out with the North Florida Inland Long-term Recovery Group, as time allowed. I helped the Economic Recovery arm of the group by applying for a grant. I also helped Jackson County with a Recovery Fair. Then, I went to Tallahassee with my friend Shareta Wright advocating for our town. When in the office, we balanced permits and grants together. When I was away, my staff balanced permits and grants for the City.

We helped people with condemnation of their homes to expedite insurance reimbursement. We began making a list of houses that need to be removed for public safety reason and requested assistance with the removal. We wrote more grants and plans, while meeting with FEMA and other national agencies regularly.

SURVIVING HURRICANE MICHAEL: A COMMUNITY'S STORY OF DEVASTATION, SURVIVAL AND HOPE DURING RECOVERY

In July I realized I had not made good on my promise to Chief Baggett to write a book. So, I sat down with my planner and scheduled out time for writing. It didn't take me long to realize that the story wasn't mine at all. It was the community's story. However, writing a community story takes much longer. I had been interviewing businesses for over a year to promote them in the local newspapers. During that time I had heard many stories about what different business owners had been through, and I then questioned what the first responders went through. This type of questioning grows exponentially. I started hearing different stories, and people were led to me through my staff. I listened to story after story and felt the hearts of the community. The hardest part of writing this book was stopping the interview process. It was impossible to include everyone, but everyone's story was important. I prayed I would include a good sample, and that the stories would help document history, while helping others to prepare for the unknown.

Left to Right: Me, Ashley, and Paula - The Municipal Development Department on Be One Day – 10/10/2019. Photo provided by Kay Dennis.

We are still very busy in the office. Now, we are working towards taking down about 50 structures destroyed by Hurricane Michael. Each of us continue to struggle with flat tires from hurricane debris. We continue to seek out ways to assist with recovery. I still hear heart breaking stories.

Left to Right: Ashley Bradie, Senator George Gainer and Me.

Conclusion

The aftermath of Hurricane Michael is more difficult for the locals, and especially the ones who are older, because they know the beauty that is lost. With children entering their early thirties, it is apparent that my children did not lose as much. However, while I was writing this book I realized, that it is the not the natural environment or the historic character that makes the town. Instead, it is the people who gathered together in love helping one another, the churches and first responders. It is the people who call Marianna and Jackson County home. While it may not be as beautiful outside as we once remembered, the people here still make Marianna and Jackson County beautiful with their loving, giving, accepting and beautiful hearts. That is why I call Marianna "Heaven on Earth". Your help is appreciated in purchasing this book. To find out how you can help more, email me at hurricanemichael101018@gmail.com.

Bibliography

Dennis, K. (2018, November 24). Marianna: Recovering Hearts Welcome Your Business. *Tallahassee Democrat, 4A.*

Dennis, K. (2018, November 27). Marianna: Recovering Hearts Welcome Your Business. *Dothan Eagle, 4A.*

Green, D. (2019, October 13). Sermon on Luke 17:11-19, Proper 23, Year C, 2019.

Masters, J. (2018). Hurricane Michael Makes Landfall in Florida Panhandle. Retrieved from https://www.wunderground.com/cat6/Potentially-Catastrophic-Hurricane-Michael-Nearing-Landfall-Florida-Panhandle.

Wikipedia contributors. (2019, November 25). Hurricane Michael. *Wikipedia, The Free Encyclopedia.* Retrieved from https://en.wikipedia.org/wiki/Hurricane_Michael.

Acknowledgments

This book is a result of interviews conducted in Marianna and Jackson County following Hurricane Michael. I am grateful for Hayes Baggett for encouraging me to record the history as told through the people who lived it. I am equally grateful for Jim Dean allowing me the time to conduct interviews.

I would like to thank my cousin Ed for encouraging me to write a book in the early 1990s. As promised the first copy is signed for you Ed. I would also like to thank all the others, who encouraged me to write over the years.

I am thankful for each person who took the time to relive and tell their stories, which in many cases were very painful. I appreciate your willingness to be vulnerable, so I could document your story for history and to help others understand.

I would like to thank Paula Livergood and Ashley Bradie for their work in setting up interviews, editing and other contributions to the book and office. Thank you Ron Swift for your technical assistance with computers, copying machines and software.

I am thankful for Ashley Bradie, Marti Vickery and Britt Dennis for editing the many versions that were provided.

Finally, I am grateful for the patience and understanding of my family, when I was busy writing at night and on weekends.

About the Author

Kay Keel Dennis was born in Marianna, Florida in 1966. She graduated from Marianna High School and Chipola College. As a young mother of two she returned to school to earn a Bachelor of Arts degree from Florida State University in Political Science and International Affairs. She would later study Urban and Regional Planning, while working as a Planner for Jackson County Board of County Commissioners. In 2005 during the time she was working as the Municipal Development Director for the City of Marianna, Kay earned two Master of Science Degrees in Business Administration and Public Administration. She became interested in how businesses and non-profits could partner with local governments to achieve higher qualities of life for local residents.

Knowing something was missing in her life, in 2016 Kay decided to pursue further education in Theology. Since that time she has earned a second Bachelor of Arts degree and is working on her Master of Arts in Theology. This was a decision Kay shared as "life changing". After Kay went back to school she began leading adult Sunday school classes, and Wednesday night church youth groups. During this time friend Wilanne Daniels shared with her the importance of actively listening to others. Kay used this skill to write articles promoting local businesses, highlighting the human side of each business, in the *Jackson County Times* and *Jackson County Floridan.*

A few days after Hurricane Michael came through Marianna, colleague and friend Hayes Baggett asked Kay to write a book about what the community had endured with the storm. Kay, a person who loves a good story and loves Marianna, listened carefully and felt what each person shared. The resulting *Surviving Hurricane Michael: A Community's Story of Devastation, Survival and Recovery,* is the first of many works to follow.

Kay continues to reside in Marianna with her husband of 32 years, Britt. The couple have two children and two grandchildren. She works for the City of Marianna in the capacity of Municipal Development Director, and enjoys reading, writing, studying and listening to stories in her spare time.

Made in the USA
Coppell, TX
29 December 2019